2012 Conference of the North American Chapter of the Association for Computational Linguistics: Human Language Technologies

(NAACL HLT 2012)

Demonstration Session

Montreal, Quebec, Canada
4 June 2012

ISBN: 978-1-62276-232-3

Printed from e-media with permission by:

Curran Associates, Inc.
57 Morehouse Lane
Red Hook, NY 12571

Some format issues inherent in the e-media version may also appear in this print version.

Printed by Curran Associates, Inc. (2012)

For permission requests, please contact the Association for Computational Linguistics at the address below.

Association for Computational Linguistics
209 N. Eighth Street
Stroudsburg, Pennsylvania 18360

Phone: 1-570-476-8006
Fax: 1-570-476-0860

acl@aclweb.org

Additional copies of this publication are available from:

Curran Associates, Inc.
57 Morehouse Lane
Red Hook, NY 12571 USA
Phone: 845-758-0400
Fax: 845-758-2634
Email: curran@proceedings.com
Web: www.proceedings.com

TABLE OF CONTENTS

Demonstrations Co-Chairs:

Aria Haghighi, Prismatic (USA)
Yaser Al-Onaizan, IBM T.J. Watson Research Center (USA)

DeSoCoRe: Detecting Source Code Re-Use across Programming Languages*

Enrique Flores, Alberto Barrón-Cedeño, Paolo Rosso, and Lidia Moreno
ELiRF, Departament of Information Systems and Computation
Universidad Politécnica de Valencia, Spain
{eflores,lbarron,prosso,lmoreno}@dsic.upv.es

Abstract

Source code re-use has become an important problem in academia. The amount of code available makes necessary to develop systems supporting education that could address the problem of detection of source code re-use. We present the DeSoCoRe tool based on techniques of Natural Language Processing (NLP) applied to detect source code re-use. DeSoCoRe compares two source codes at the level of methods or functions even when written in different programming languages. The system provides an understandable output to the human reviewer in order to help a teacher to decide whether a source code is re-used.

1 Introduction

Identifying whether a work has been re-used has received increasing interest in recent years. As for documents in natural language, the amount of source code on Internet is increasing; facilitating the re-use of all or part of previously implemented programs.[1] If no reference to the original work is included, plagiarism would be committed. The interest for detecting software re-use is great discouraging academic cheating.

Many online tools exist for detecting re-use in text, such as Churnalism[2]. To the best of our knowledge the unique online service to detecting re-use in source code is JPlag[3]. This tool can process different programming languages, but at monolingual level.

This paper presents the DeSoCoRe tool for detection source code re-use across programming languages. We estimate the similarity between two source codes independently of the programming language using NLP techniques. In fact, programming languages are similar to natural languages; both can be represented as strings of symbols (characters, words, phrases, etc.).

DeSoCoRe aims at supporting a reviewer in the process of detecting highly similar source code functions. It allows to visualize the matches detected between two source codes d and d_q. The programs are represented as a graph. An edge exists between a function in d_q and a function in d if re-use between them is suspected. The code chunks are displayed to the user for further review. With the information provided, the reviewer can decide whether a fragment is re-used or not.

2 Related Work

In the previous section we mention only one online tool but many research works for source code re-use detection exist. Two main approaches have been explored: content-based and structure-based.

Content-based approaches are based on analysis of strings within the source codes. The pioneering work of (Halstead, 1972) is based on units countings. He counts the total number of operands, total number of different operands and number of operators, among others.

* Screencast available at: *http://vimeo.com/33148670*. The tool is available at: *http://memex2.dsic.upv.es:8080/DeSoCoRe/*

[1] Source code re-use is often allowed, thanks to licenses as those of Creative Commons (*http://creativecommons.org/*)

[2] *http://churnalism.com/*

[3] *https://www.ipd.uni-karlsruhe.de/jplag/*

Proceedings of the NAACL-HLT 2012: Demonstration Session, pages 1–4,
Montréal, Canada, June 3-8, 2012.

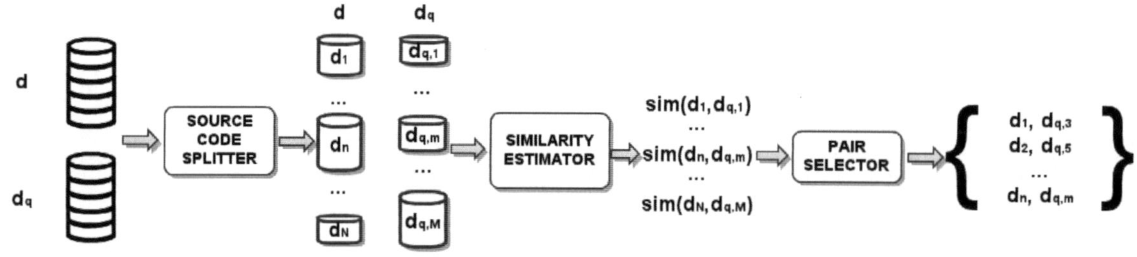

Figure 1: Architecture of DeSoCoRe tool. The source code d has N functions, and d_q has M functions. Each function of d is compared against all the functions of d_q.

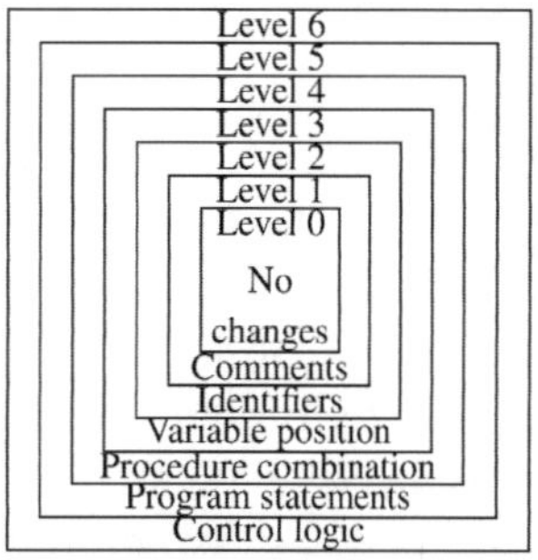

Figure 2: Levels of program modifications in a plagiarism spectrum proposed by Faidhi and Robinson.

Structure-based approaches, the most used up to date, focus the analysis on the code structure (execution tree) in order to estimate the level of similarity between two source codes. A seminal model is the proposed by (Whale, 1990b). This approach codifies branches, repeats, and statements in order to estimate the similarity between two programs. This model has inspired several other tools, such as Plague (Whale, 1990a) and its further developments YAP[1,2,3] (Wise, 1992).

JPlag (Prechelt et al., 2002) combines both approaches. In the first stage, it exploits syntax in order to normalize variables and function names. In the second stage, it looks for common strings between programs. This work attempts to detect several levels of obfuscation[4]. It achieves better results than JPlag for highly obfuscated cases but worst results with low degree of obfuscation.

JPlag is able to detect source code re-use in different programming languages although at monolingual level; that is, one programming language at a time. None of the reviewed approaches is able to perform cross-language analysis. To the best of our knowledge the only approach to analyze cross-language source code re-use is the one of (Arwin and Tahaghoghi, 2006). Instead of processing source code, this approach compares intermediate code produced by a compiler which includes noise in the detection process. The comparison is in fact monolingual and compiler dependent. The resulting tool, Xplag, allows to compute similarity between codes in Java and C.

[4]Obfuscation in re-use can be considered as reformulation, which inserts noise.

3 Architecture

As shown in Figure 1, DeSoCoRe consists of three general modules. As input user gives a pair of source codes (d, d_q). The source code splitter is responsible for dividing the codes in functions. To split each code into functions we have developed syntactic analyzers for Python and for C syntax family language: C, C++, Java, C#, etc.

The next module compares the functions of d_q against the functions of d. To make this comparison we have divided the module into three sub-modules: (*a*) *Pre-processing*: line breaks, tabs and spaces removal as well as case folding; (*b*) *Features extraction*: character n-grams extraction, weighting based on normalized term frequency (tf); and (*c*) *Comparison*: a cosine similarity estimation. As output, we obtain a similarity value in the range [0-1] for all the pairs of functions between the source codes.

We carried out several experiments in order to find the best way to detect re-use in source codes. These experiments were inspired by what proposed in (Faidhi and Robinson, 1987). They describes the modifications that a programmer makes to hide the re-use of source code as Figure 2 shows. These levels are: (*i*) changes in comments and indentation;

(*ii*) changes in identifiers; (*iii*) changes in declarations; (*iv*) changes in program modules; (*v*) changes in the program statements; (*vi*) changes in the decision logic. As result of these experiments we obtained best configuration of our system to use the entire source code and to apply 3-grams (Flores et al., 2011).

Once the similarity value has been calculated for all the possible pairs, the pair selector decides what pairs are good source re-used candidates. This module has to discard the pairs which have obtained a similarity value lower than a threshold established by the user. As output DeSoCoRe returns the suspicious pairs that have been re-used.

4 Demonstration

In order to interact with our developed system, we provide a Java applet interface. It is divided in two interfaces: (*i*) input screen: which allows the user for inserting two source codes, select their programming language and additionally to select a value for the similarity threshold;[5] (*ii*) output screen: which shows the results divided in two sections: (*a*) a graphical visualization of the codes; and (*b*) a plain text representation of the codes. In the first section we have used the Prefuse Library[6] in order to draw a graph representing the similarity between the functions of the source codes. The painted graph consists of two red nodes which represent each source code. Their functions are represented by purple nodes and connected to the source code node with edges. If any of these functions has been selected by the system as re-used, its nodes will be connected to a node from the other source code.

Finally, a node is marked in red if it composes a potential case of reuse. When a function is pointed, the plain text section displays the source code. Also, if this function has any potential case of re-use, the function and the potential re-used function will be shown to perform a manual review of the codes. In order to be introduced to DeSoCoRe an example is provided and can be accessed clicking on the *Example* button. Figure 3 shows an example of two supicious source codes: one in C++ and one in Java. The user is able to start the estimation of similarity clicking on *Estimate!* button.

After similarity estimation, the result is displayed as in Figure 3(a). For exploratory purpouses, example source codes are available through the *Example* button. The user is able to start the estimation of similarity clicking on *Estimate!* button. Figure 3(b) shows an example of potential cases of reuse. The function *crackHTTPAuth* is selected in the right source code node, and the selected as possible case of re-use is marked on orange. The plain text representation of these two parts of source code shows that they are practically identical.

5 Conclusions and Future Work

The main goal of this research work is to provide a helpful tool for source code reviewers in order to help them to decide wheter or not a source code has been re-used. DeSoCoRe is the first online tool which it can detect source code re-use across languages as far of our knowledge.

We have developed a methodology for detecting source code re-use across languages, and have shown their functionality by presenting DeSoCoRe tool, which works between and within programming languages. This makes our tool a valuable cross-lingual source code detector. DeSoCoRe allows comparing source codes written in Python, Java and C syntax family languages: C, C++ or C#. We plan in the next future to extend its functionality to other common programming languages. As future work we aim at allowing for the comparison at fragment level, where a fragment is considered a part of a function, a group of functions.

Acknowledgments

This work was done in the framework of the VLC/ CAMPUS Microcluster on Multimodal Interaction in Intelligent Systems and it has been partially funded by the European Commission as part of the WiQ-Ei IRSES project (grant no. 269180) within the FP 7 Marie Curie People Framework, and by MICINN as part of the Text-Enterprise 2.0 project (TIN2009-13391-C04-03) within the Plan I+D+i. The research work of the second author is funded by the CONACyT-Mexico 192021 grant.

[5] In agreement with (Flores et al., 2011), the default threshold for C-like languages (C, C++, Java...) is 0.8.

[6] Software tools for creating rich interactive data visualizations (*http://prefuse.org/*)

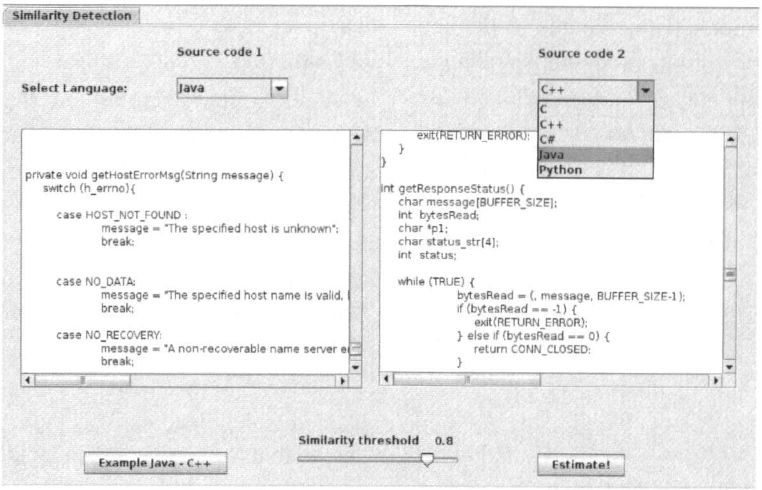

(a) Input screen: user have to select each language manually.

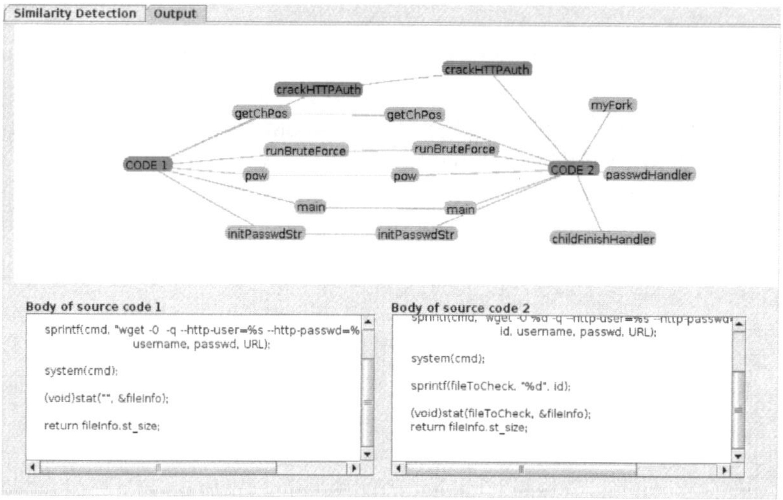

(b) Output screen: the re-used functions are connected using an edge and their codes are shown in the text areas below.

Figure 3: Screenshot of the interface of DeSoCoRe.

References

C. Arwin and S. Tahaghoghi. 2006. Plagiarism detection across programming languages. *Proceedings of the 29th Australian Computer Science Conference*, 48:277–286.

J. Faidhi and S. Robinson. 1987. An empirical approach for detecting program similarity and plagiarism within a university programming enviroment. *Computers and Education*, 11:11–19.

E. Flores, A. Barrón-Cedeño, P. Rosso and L. Moreno. 2011. Towards the Detection of Cross-Language Source Code Reuse. *Proceedings 16th International Conference on Applications of Natural Language to Information Systems, NLDB-2011, Springer-Verlag, LNCS(6716)*, pp. 250–253.

M. Halstead. 1972. Naturals laws controlling algorithm structure?. *SIGPLAN Noticies*, 7(2).

L. Prechelt, G. Malpohl and M. Philippsen. 2002. Finding plagiarisms among a set of programs with JPlag. *Journal of Universal Computer Science*, 8(11):1016–1038.

G. Whale. 1990. Identification of program similarity in large populations. *The Computer Journal*, 33(2).

G. Whale. 1990. Software metrics and plagiarism detection. *Journal of Systems and Software*, 13:131–138.

M. Wise. 1992. Detection of similarities in student programs: Yaping may be preferable to Plagueing. *"Proceedings of the 23th SIGCSE Technical Symposium.*

A Graphical User Interface for Feature-Based Opinion Mining

Pedro Balage Filho
University of Wolverhampton
pedrobalage@gmail.com

Caroline Brun
Xerox Research Centre Europe
Caroline.Brun@xrce.xerox.com

Gilbert Rondeau
Xerox Research Centre Europe
Gilbert.Rondeau@xrce.xerox.com

Abstract

In this paper, we present XOpin, a graphical user interface that have been developed to provide a smart access to the results of a feature-based opinion detection system, build on top of a parser.

1 Introduction

Opinion mining (or sentiment analysis) arouses great interest in recent years both in academia and industry. Very broadly, sentiment analysis aims to detect the attitude of a person toward a specific topic expressed in natural language and to evaluate the polarity of what is been expressed, i.e., whether it is positive or negative. With the emergence of the Web 2.0, i.e., forums, blogs, web sites compiling consumer reviews on various subjects, there is a huge amount of documents containing information expressing opinions: the "user generated content". This constitutes a very important data source for monitoring various applications (business intelligence, product and service benchmarking, technology watch). Numerous research works at the crossroads of NLP and data mining are focusing on the problem of opinion detection and mining. In this paper, we present the advanced research prototype we have designed: it consists in an integration of a feature-based opinion detection system together with a graphical user interface providing to the end-user a smart access to the results of the opinion detection.

We first present an overview of sentiment analysis. Then, we detail the system we have developed, in particular the graphical user interface, and conclude.

2 Analyzing Sentiment in Texts

Sentiment Analysis plays a very important role to help people to find better products or to compare product characteristics. For the consumer, a good interface allows to navigate, compare and identify the main characteristics of the products or companies. For the company, it is interesting to know the customer preferences. It is an essential step to optimize marketing campaigns and to develop new features in products.

Despite the increase of interest in sentiment analysis, many tools do not pay much attention to the user interface aspects. These aspects are very important in order to satisfy the user needs.

In the literature, we find some different ways to aggregate and represent the summary information from a collection of texts annotated with sentiment. For instance, Gamon et al. (2005) use colors to display the general assessment of product features. The system shows the reviews as boxes, where the box size indicates the number of mentions of that topic and the color indicates the average sentiment it contains. This interface allows having a quick glance about the most important topics and the sentiment expressed.

Another display idea is presented in the Opinion Observer (Liu et al., 2005). In this system, a bar shows the polarity related with each product and each feature. The portions of the bar above and below a horizontal line represent the amount of positive and negative reviews. For example, in a cell phone domain, the sentiment associated with features like LCD, battery, reception and speaker are used to compare the relevance of one product in opposite to another.

Morinaga et al. (2002) present an interface where the sentiment information is represented by the degrees of association between products and opinion-indicative terms. The author uses principal component analysis to produce a two-dimensional visualization where the terms and products are plotted indicating the relatedness among the points.

In the internet, we can find many systems and companies related with sentiment analysis. For example, the company Lexalytics has in its website

Proceedings of the NAACL-HLT 2012: Demonstration Session, pages 5–8,
Montréal, Canada, June 3-8, 2012. ©2012 Association for Computational Linguistics

an available demo[1] for sentiment detection. This demo shows an interface which highlights positive and negative words in the text. The interface also shows entities, categories associated, a summary and the top terms.

The RankSpeed [2] is a website for product comparison. The website includes in the search the sentiment associated with each product. In the interface, the user can input a list of sentiment words, like "excellent", "cool", "easy" or "powerful" that the system will organize the results according the frequency of those words in reviews related to the products.

The Stock Sonar[3] has a timeline chart as the main interface. In this timeline, both positive and negative sentiments are displayed throughout time. The sentiments are retrieved from real-time news associated with a particular company. In the same timeline, it is possible to follow-up the increase or decrease of the stock prices for that company in that period of time. In this application, the sentiment is used to forecast market actions such as buy and sell stocks.

All those systems presented relevant components for a powerful opinion mining interface, but none of them deliver a full interface to explore the multi-aspects in opinion mining. For us, a complete system should provide both single and multi-document visualization, work on the feature level classification, and produce an integrated interface to browse, navigate, filter and visualize files, features and sentiment tendencies. In the following section, we present XOpin, a graphical user interface that have been developed to provide the characteristics described.

3 The System and its Interface

To detect opinions in texts, our system relies on a robust incremental parser, XIP, (Ait-Mokhtar and Chanod 2002), specifically adapted for opinion detection. The system extracts opinions related to the main concepts commented in reviews (e.g. products, movies, books...), but also on features associated to these products (such as certain characteristics of the products, their price, associated services, etc...). More precisely, we adopt the formal representation of an opinion proposed by Liu (2010): an opinion is represented as a five place predicate of the form $(o_j, f_{jk}, so_{ijkl}, h_i, t_l)$, where: o_j is the target of the opinion (the main concept), f_{jk} is a feature associated to the object o_j, so_{ijkl} is the value (positive or negative) of the opinion expressed by the opinion holder h_i about the feature f_{jk}, h_i is the opinion holder, t_l is the time when the opinion is expressed.

We use the robust parser to extract, using syntactic relations already extracted by a general dependency grammar, semantic relations instantiating this model. Other systems use syntactic dependencies to link source and target of the opinion, for example in Kim and Hovy (2006). Our system belongs to this family, as we believe that syntactic processing of complex phenomena (negation, comparison and anaphora) is a necessary step to perform feature-based opinion mining. Another specificity of our system is a two level architecture based on a generic level, applicable to any domain, and on a domain-dependent level, adapted for each sub-domain of application. Regarding evaluation, the relations of opinion extracted by the system have been used to train a SVM classifier in order to assess the system's ability to correctly classify user's reviews as positive or negative. Results are quite satisfying, as they show 93% of accuracy to classify reviews about printers and 89% of accuracy to classify reviews about movies (Brun, 2011).

The XOpin Interface was developed to provide an easy way to allow the user to explore the results of this sentiment analysis system. The interface provides a graphical environment that allows the user to browse, navigate, filter and visualize the necessary information in a collection of texts.

The tool accepts as input pure text files or xml files. The xml files follow a specific format which allows the system to retrieve metadata information. It is also possible to retrieve web pages from the web. The tool offers the possibility to retrieve a single webpage, given the URL, or a collection of pages by crawling. To crawl, for example, reviews webpages, the user need to setup some crawling and information extraction rules defined by a template in the configuration file. The files retrieved from the web are converted in xml format, which allows preserving the metadata information. As an example, Figure 1 shows the

[1]http://www.lexalytics.com/webdemo
[2]http://www.rankspeed.com/
[3]http://www.thestocksonar.com/

organization of this xml file from a review retrieved from the website epinions.com (http://www.epinions.com).

```
<review>
  <source value="http://..." />
  <domain value="Printers"/>
  <brand value="Hewlett Packard"/>
  <product value=" Hewlett Packard 6500A"/>
  <opinion_holder value="user_name"/>
  <review_date value="01/Dec/2011"/>
  <opinion value="Yes"/>
  <review_stars value="5"/>
  <review_popularity value="10"/>
  <textblock layout="title">
        Review Title
  </textblock>
  <textblock layout="summary">
        Review Summary
  </textblock>
  <textblock layout="text">
        Review Free Comment
  </textblock>
</review>
```

Figure 1. Organization of the XML file

The tag *source* keeps the URL from where the review was extracted. The tags domain, brand and product keep the specific data about to the product. The tag *opinion_holder* keeps the name of the user who wrote the review. The tag *review_date* keeps the date when the review was written. The tag *opinion* keeps the user general assessment about the product. In the website epinions.com, the user can assess the product as recommended (Yes) or not recommended (No). The tag *review_stars* contains the number of stars the user attributed to the product. The tag *review_popularity* keeps the number of positive evaluations (thumbsUp) of this particular review by the other users. In the reviews from the website epinions.com we don't have this assessment, so this number represents how many users assigned to trust in this reviewer. The tags *textblock* contain the text for the sections title, summary and review.

After loading a file or a corpus into the tool, the texts are showed in a tree structure in the left panel. A hierarchical structure allows the user to have the corpus organized as a conventional folder structure. In this way, it is possible to analyze the texts inside a specific folder and also to include the texts in the subfolders inside.

To analyze this data, the tool presents three main views: text, timeline and comparison. In the text view, negative terms, positive terms and entities present in the text are highlighted. The purpose of this view is to provide a visual assessment about the sentiment expressed in the text. If the text was loaded by crawling or by an xml file, the metadata is also displayed. Figure 2 shows an example of reviews collected from the website epinions.com, in the category printers.

As said before, XOpin is able to identify the predicates associated with each sentiment and the category it belongs. For example, in the sentence "This printer gives excellent quality color", the tool highlights the positive sentiment "excellent", the predicate associated "color" and organize this predicate into the category color. This predicate categorization depends of the sub-domain architecture level.

This classification is very important to present an organized summary about which category is most positive and with is most negative in the text. The right panel shows this information.

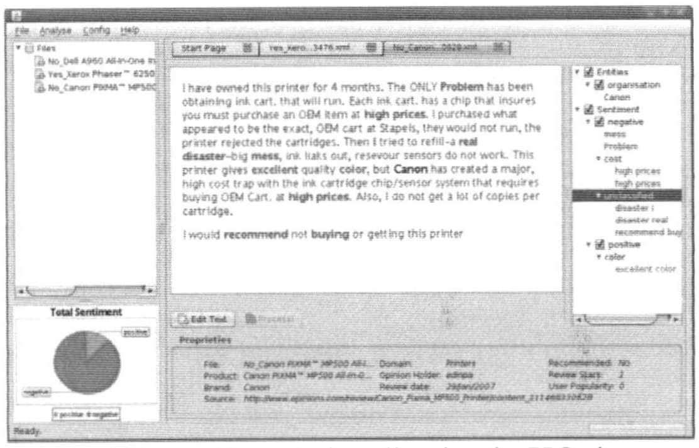

Figure 2. Text visualization in XOpin

The timeline screen (Figure 3) offers the user the option to analyze a corpus of texts organized by time, for example, reviews crawled from the web. In this way, the user can create flexible and interesting views about the products and features found in the corpus.

The timeline shows the total of positive and negative words in the texts for a given date. With this information and a larger enough corpus of reviews it is possible to have a big picture about the user preferences and dissatisfactions.

The timeline also offers the possibility to show the positive and negative lines for specific brands, products and features in a determined timespan. Filters can remove anything that it is not useful and create a pure visualization about what the user need to see. The left and bottom panels offer options to create those views.

These views can show an evolution in the user's perspective in respect to some new improvement in the product. For example, in a marketing campaign, the company can evaluate the user behavior about the product price.

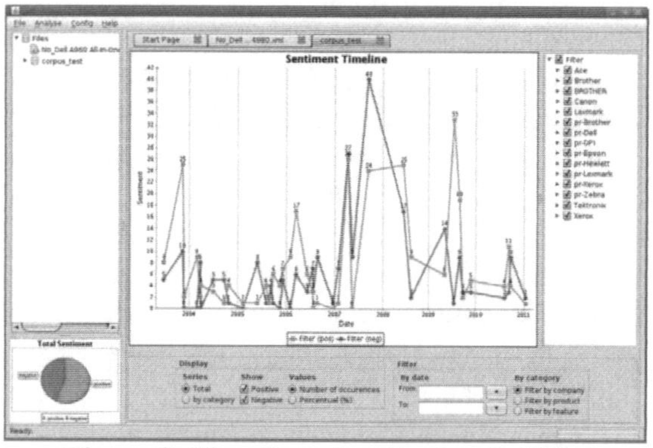

Figure 3. Timeline visualization in XOpin

The comparison view (Figure 4) allows the user to compare side by side different product features in a collection of texts. In this view, the user has the main predicate associated with each feature and the number of positive or negative occurrences. This is interesting in order to have a big picture about what the users are commenting in positive or negative aspects for each feature.

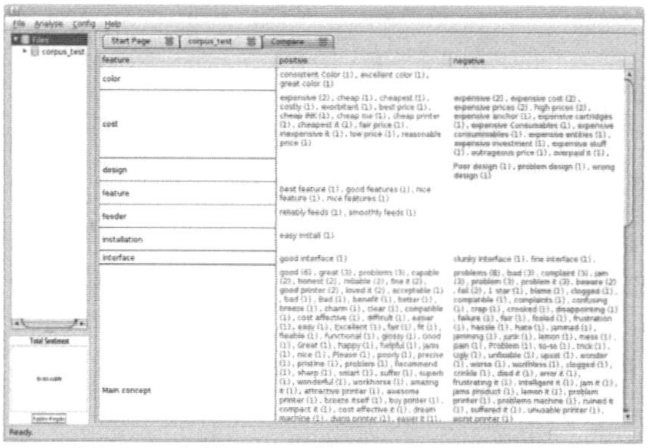

Figure 4. Feature Comparison in XOpin

4 Conclusion

This paper presents an NLP-based opinion mining advanced prototype integrating a dedicated graphical user interface which provides a smart access to the results of the opinion detection. The interface has been build in order to ensure advanced functionalities such as opinion highlighting on text and features, timeline visualization and feature comparison. The system has been demonstrated to potential customers and it received a good feedback. In our assessment, the integrated features provided by the system increased the usability in the data exploration for a reviews corpus compared against other products.

References

Salah Ait-Mokthar, Jean-Pierre Chanod. Robustness beyond Shallowness: Incremental Dependency Parsing. *Special Issue of NLE Journal*, 2002.

Caroline Brun. Detecting Opinions Using Deep Syntactic Analysis. In *Proceedings of the Recent Advances in Natural Language Processing (RANLP)*, Hissar, Bulgaria, September 12-14, 2011.

Michael Gamon, Anthony Aue, Simon Corston-Oliver, and Eric Ringger. Pulse: Mining customer opinions from free text. In *Proceedings of the International Symposium on Intelligent Data Analysis (IDA)*, number 3646 in Lecture Notes in Computer Science, pages 121–132, 2005.

Kim, S.M. and E.H. Hovy. Identifying and Analyzing Judgment Opinions. *Proceedings of the Human Language Technology/HLT-NAACL*. New York, 2006.

Bing Liu, Minqing Hu, and Junsheng Cheng. Opinion observer: Analyzing and comparing opinions on the web. In *Proceedings of WWW*, 2005.

Bing Liu. *Sentiment Analysis and Subjectivity*, Chapter of Handbook of Natural Language Processing, 2nd edition, 2010.

Satoshi Morinaga, Kenji Yamanishi, Kenji Tateishi, and Toshikazu Fukushima.Mining product reputations on the web. In *Proceedings of the ACM SIGKDD Conference on Knowledge Discovery and Data Mining (KDD)*, pages 341–349, 2002.

Navigating Large Comment Threads With CoFi

Christine Doran, Guido Zarrella and John C. Henderson
The MITRE Corporation
Bedford, MA
{cdoran,jzarrella,jhndrsn}@mitre.org

Abstract

Comment threads contain fascinating and useful insights into public reactions, but are challenging to read and understand without computational assistance. We present a tool for exploring large, community-created comments threads in an efficient manner.

1 Introduction

The comments made on blog posts and news articles provide both immediate and ongoing public reaction to the content of the post or article. When a given site allows users to respond to each other ("threaded" responses), the comment sets become a genuine public conversation. However, this information can be difficult to access. Comments are typically not indexed by search engines, the volume is often enormous, and threads may continue to be added to over months or even years. This makes it hard to find particular information of interest (say, a mention of a particular company in a set of thousands of YouTube comments), or to understand the gist of the discussion at a high-level.

Our goal in this work was to create a simple tool which would allow people to rapidly ingest useful information contained in large community-created comment threads, where the volume of data precludes manual inspection. To this end, we created CoFi (**Co**mment **Fi**lter), a language-independent, web-based interactive browser for single comment threads.

2 How CoFi works

For a given set of comments, we create a distinct CoFi instance. Each instance is over a natural data set, e.g. all comments from a particular discussion group, comments attached to an individual news article, or tweets resulting from a topical search. Creating a CoFi instance has three steps: harvesting the comments, clustering the comments, and responding to user interactions while they visualize and navigate (sorting and filtering) the dataset.

2.1 Harvesting the data

Our comments are harvested from individual web sites. These need not be in English, or even in a single language. Typically, sites use proprietary javascript to present comments. Each web site has a unique interface and formatting to serve the comments to web browsers, and there is no general purpose tool to gather comments everywhere. The CoFi approach has been to factor this part of the problem into one harvesting engine per web site. Some sites provide an API that simplifies the problem of harvesting comments that contain particular keywords. On other sites, there seems to be no reliable alternative to developer ingenuity when it comes to altering the harvesting engines to accommodate data formats. Thus, we note that the harvesting activity is only *semi*-automated.

2.2 Clustering the data

Once harvesting is complete, the rest of the process is automatic. Clusters are generated and labeled using a pipeline of machine learning tools. The open source package MALLET provides many of our document ingestion and clustering components (McCallum, 2002). Our processing components are language-independent and can be used with non-English or mixed language data sets.

Specifically, we use a combination of Latent Dirichlet Allocation (LDA), K-Means clustering, and calculation of mutual information. LDA models each document (aka comment) as a mixture of latent topics, which are in turn comprised of a probability distribution over words (Chen, 2011, gives a good overview). It's an unsupervised algorithm that performs approximate inference. The topics it infers are the ones that best explain the statistical distributions of words observed in the

Proceedings of the NAACL-HLT 2012: Demonstration Session, pages 9–12,
Montréal, Canada, June 3-8, 2012.

data. It is highly parallelizable and so it scales well to very large data sets. In practice we ask LDA to search for *5k* topics, where *k* is the number of clusters we will eventually display to the user.

The second step is to perform K-Means clustering on the documents, where the documents are represented as a mixture of LDA topics as described above, and the clustering chooses *k* clusters that minimize the differences between documents in the cluster while maximizing the difference between documents that are not in the same clusters. This step is fast, in part because of the fact that we have already reduced the number of input features down to *5k* (rather than having one feature for each word observed in the entire dataset.)

Finally, we give the clusters titles by performing a calculation of mutual information (MI) for each word or bigram in each cluster. Specifically, clustering terms (both words and bigrams) that occur frequently in one cluster but rarely in other clusters will receive high scores. The terms with the highest MI scores are used as cluster labels.

One significant advantage of this completely unsupervised approach is that CoFi is more robust to the language of comment data, e.g. grammatical and spelling inconsistency, informal language, which are a challenge for rule-based and supervised NLP tools.

In addition to the machine-generated topic clusters, CoFi allows user-defined topics. These are search terms and topic labels hand-created by a domain expert. CoFi partitions the comments into machine-generated topics and *also* assigns each comment to any of the matching predefined topics. This approach is useful for domain experts, enabling them to quickly find things they already know they want while allowing them to also take advantage of unexpected topics which emerge from the system clustering.

2.3 Creating the visualizations

CoFi uses the **`JQuery`**, **`Flot`**, and **`g.Raphael`** javascript libraries to provide a dynamic, responsive interface. When the user visits a CoFi URL, the data is downloaded into their browser which then computes the visualization elements locally, allowing fast response times and offline access to the data. The **`JQuery`** library is central to all of the javascript processing that CoFi performs, and ensures that all features of the interface are cross-compatible with major browser versions.

The interface provides the ability to drill down further into any data, allowing the user to click on any aspect of the analysis to obtain more detail. Since the visualization is calculated locally, the software can create dynamically updated timelines that show the user how any subset of their data has changed over time.

It is also important to prioritize all data presented to the user, allowing them to focus on the most useful documents first. CoFi applies an automatic summarization technique to perform relevance sorting. We evaluated several state-of-the-art automatic document summarization techniques and settled on a Kullback-Leibler divergence inspired by techniques described in Kumar et al. (2009). The "relevance" sort relies on a measure of how representative each comment is relative to the entire collection of comments that the user is viewing at the time. This allows us to rapidly rank tens of thousands of comments in the order of their relevance to a summary. Several of the approaches we tested were chosen from among the leaders of NIST's 2004 Document Understanding Conference (DUC) summarization evaluation. Many of them used slight variants of KL divergence for sentence scoring. We also implemented Lin & Bilmes' (2010) Budgeted Maximization of Submodular Functions system, which performed best according to the DUC evaluation. However, even after applying a scaling optimization inspired by the "buckshot" technique of Cutting et al. (1992) the processing speed was still too slow for dealing with datasets containing more than 10000 small documents. The KL divergence approach scales linearly in the number of comments while still offering cutting edge qualitative performance. This means that the calculation can be done on the fly in javascript in the browser when the user requests a relevance sort. This allows CoFi to tailor the results to whatever sub-selection of data is currently being displayed. For CoFi's typical use cases this computation can be completed in under 2 seconds.

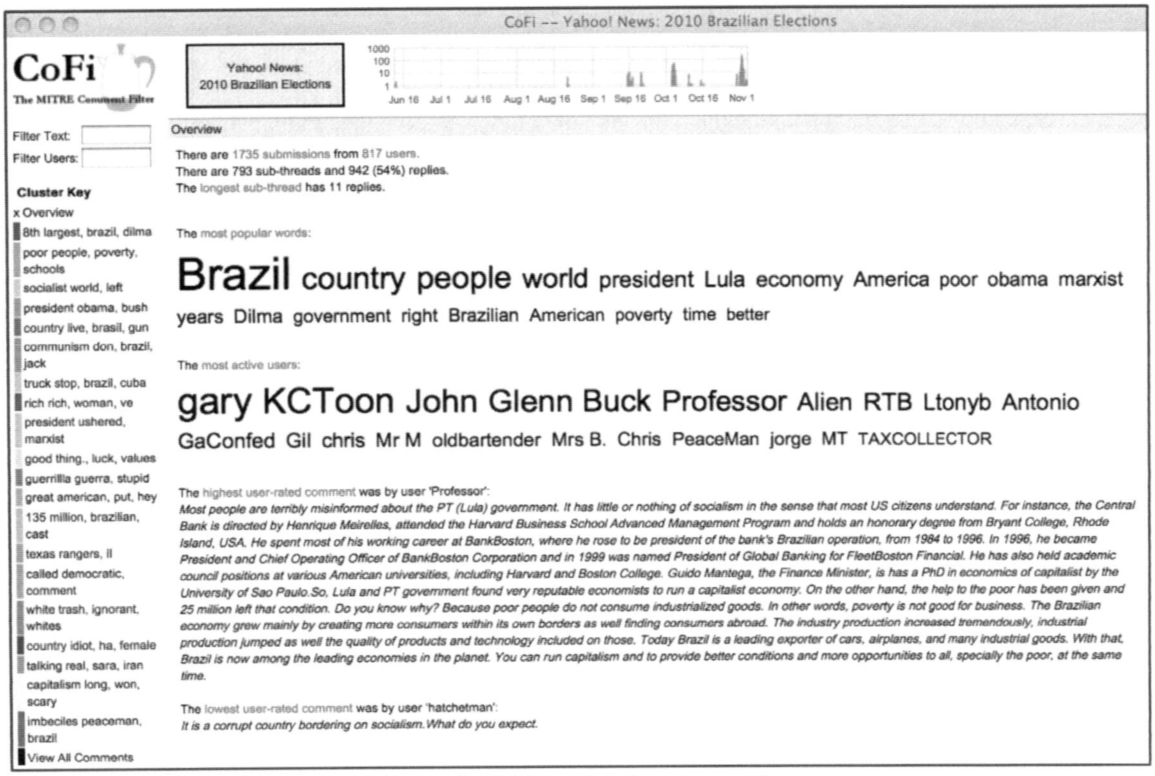

Figure 1: CoFi top level summary view

3 The CoFi Interface

CoFi takes a set of comments and produces the interactive summary you see in Figure 1. CoFi works best when a user is operating with between 200 and 10,000 comments. With small numbers of comments, there may not be enough data for CoFi to find interesting topic clusters. With very large numbers of comments, a user's web browser may struggle to display all comments while maintaining sufficient responsiveness.

The raw data is available for inspection in many ways. The summary screen in Figure 1 presents a list of automatically-discovered clusters on the left-hand side (typically 10-30, this is a parameter of the clustering algorithm), the posting volume timeline on the top, and some overall statistics and characteristic words and posters in the middle. The user can return to this view at any point using the *Overview* button. At the top of the page, CoFi presents the total number of comments and participants, and a summary of the level of threading, which is a good indicator of how interactive the data set is. Where community ratings appear on a site, we also present the highest and lowest rated comments (this is solely based on the community rating, and not on our relevance calculation). In the middle of the display are two hyperlinked word clouds containing the highest frequency words and users. Selecting one of the top words or users has the same effect as searching for that term in one of the *Search* boxes—both of these approaches will present the user with matching comments with the term highlighted, and color coding to indicate cluster membership. The links from most popular words and most active users bring up a multi-graph view as in Figure 3.

Each time a set of comments is selected, either via a cluster, full text search, or filtering on a particular commenter, the set is presented to the user in a sorted order with the comments most representative of the set ordered above those that are less representative. In this way, the user can quickly get a handle on what the set is about without reading all of the items in detail. The comments can also be sorted into the original temporal order, which can be useful to see how a comment thread evolves over time, or to view an original comment and threaded replies in a nested ordering. Figure 2 shows a single cluster in CoFi. The full thread timeline now has a red overlay for the selected subset of comments.

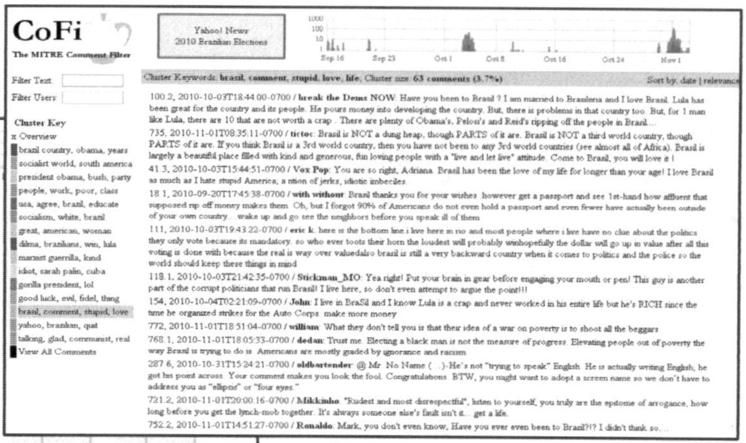

Figure 2: Single cluster view

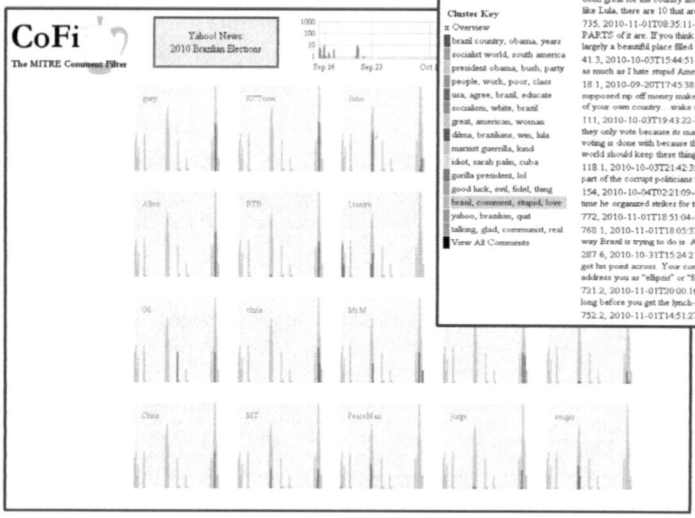

Figure 3: The "small multiples" view of frequent contributors

At the bottom of the cluster lists, there is a *View All Comments* option. Sorting the entire set by relevance gives a good snapshot of most and least useful comments in the thread. From any of the views, clicking on a user name will display all comments from that user, and clicking on the comment ID will present that sub-thread; top-level comments are numbered X, while replies are labeled X.X. The CoFi interface also allows the user to export individual comments, marking those comments as having been "handled" and routed to a particular person. This makes it easier to incrementally process comments as they arrive.

We have applied CoFi to 72 distinct data sets, including forum discussions, news article, blog and YouTube comments, Twitter and comments on regulatory changes submitted to government offices via Regulations.gov. These last documents are much longer than those CoFi was intended to handle, but CoFi was nonetheless able to support interesting analysis. In one instance, we identified a clear case of "astroturfing" (fake grassroots movement) based on the CoFi clusters.

Acknowledgements

Over the course of this project, many people have supported our work. We'd particularly like to thank Mark Maybury, Robert Peller at USSOUTHCOM, and Marty Ryan, Robert Battle and Nathan Vuong at the MITRE Miami site. This technical data was produced for the U. S. Government under Contract No. W15P7T-11-C-F600, and is subject to the Rights in Technical Data-Noncommercial Items clause at DFARS 252.227-7013 (NOV 1995).

References

Chen, Edwin (2011). Introduction to Latent Direchlet Allocation, http://blog.echen.me/2011/08/22/introduction-to-latent-dirichlet-allocation/#comments

Cutting, D., Karger, D., Pedersen, J., and Tukey, J. (1992). Scatter/Gather: a cluster-based approach to browsing large document collections. *Proceedings of 15th Annual International ACM SIGIR conference,* New York, NY, USA, 318-329

Kumar, C., P. Pingali, and V. Verma (2009). Estimating Risk Of Picking a Sentence for Document Summarization. *Proceedings of CICLing 2009*, LNCS 5449, 571-581.

Lin, H. and Bilmes, J. (2010). Multi-document summarization via budgeted maximization of submodular functions. *Proceedings of Human Language Technologies 2010*, Los Angeles, CA, USA, 912-920.

McCallum, Andrew Kachites (2002). MALLET: A Machine Learning for Language Toolkit.

Mishne, Gilard and Natalie Glance (2006). Leave a reply: An Analysis of Weblog Comments. *In Workshop on the Weblogging Ecosystem*, 15th International World Wide Web Conference, May.

SurfShop: combing a product ontology with topic model results for online window-shopping.

Zofia Stankiewicz and **Satoshi Sekine**
Rakuten Institute of Technology, New York
215 Park Avenue South
New York, NY 10003, USA
{zofia.stankiewicz, satoshi.b.sekine}@mail.rakuten.com

Abstract

At present, online shopping is typically a search-oriented activity where a user gains access to products which best match their query. Instead, we propose a *surf-oriented* online shopping paradigm, which links associated products allowing users to "wander around" the online store and enjoy browsing a variety of items. As an initial step in creating this experience, we constructed a prototype of an online shopping interface which combines product ontology information with topic model results to allow users to explore items from the food and kitchen domain. As a novel task for topic model application, we also discuss possible approaches to the task of selecting the best product categories to illustrate the hidden topics discovered for our product domain.

1 Introduction

Query based search remains the primary method of access to large collections of data. However, new interfacing options offered by mobile and touchscreen applications lead to decreased reliance on typed search queries. This trend further fuels the need for technologies which allow users to browse and explore large amounts of data from a variety of viewpoints. Online store product databases are a representative example of such a data source. At present, online shopping is typically a search-oriented activity. Aside from suggestions of closely matching products from a recommender system, internet shoppers have little opportunity to *look around* an online store and explore a variety of related items. This observation led us to define a novel task of creating a *surf-oriented* online shopping interface which facilitates browsing and access to multiple types of products. We created the prototype *SurfShop* application in order to test whether we can combine knowledge from a product ontology with topic modeling for a better browsing experience.

Our aim is to design an application which offers access to a variety of products, while providing a coherent and interesting presentation. While the product ontology provides information on product types which are semantically close (for example *spaghetti* and *penne*), it does not provide information about associations such as *pasta* and *tomato sauce*, which may be mentioned implicitly in product descriptions. In order to obtain semantically varied product groupings from the data we integrated topic model results into the application to display products which are related through hidden topics.

The data used for this project consists of a snapshot from the product database of a Japanese Internet shopping mall Rakuten Ichiba obtained in April 2011[1]. We limited our prototype application to the food and kitchen domain consisting of approximately 4 million products. The textual information available for each product includes a title and a short description. Furthermore, each product is assigned to a leaf category in the product hierarchy tree.

We use standard LDA (Blei et al., 2003) as the topic model and our prototype can be treated as an example of applied topic modeling. Although there exist browsers of document collections based

[1] For a version of Rakuten product data made available for research purposes see http://rit.rakuten.co.jp/rdr/index_en.html.

Proceedings of the NAACL-HLT 2012: Demonstration Session, pages 13–16,
Montréal, Canada, June 3-8, 2012.

on topic modeling [2], they have been constructed as direct model result visualizations. In contrast, we incorporate the LDA results into the output by combining them with product category information and search to produce a full blown application with a topic model serving as one of its components. We provide a more detailed overview of the entire system in section 2.

In LDA literature, the topics discovered by the model are typically represented by top n most probable words for a given topic. In integrating topic model results into our application we faced a challenge of creating theme pages which correspond to hidden topics, and selecting product categories which best illustrate a given topic. In section 3 we discuss a preliminary evaluation of the application's theme pages which suggests that combining topic knowledge with ontology structure can lead to more coherent product category groupings, and that topic interpretation and labeling based solely on top n words may not be sufficient for some applied tasks. We conclude by summarizing plans for further development of our prototype.

2 System overview

The initial input to the *SurfShop* system consists of a product database and a product ontology with node labels. All products were indexed for fast retrieval by the application[3]. A chart of application components is presented in Figure1.

Raw product descriptions from our data would constitute a large corpus including meta-data such as shipping or manufacturer information, which are not relevant to our task. Thus, fitting a topic model over this corpus is not guaranteed to provide useful information about related product types. Therefore, we decided to aggregate the product information into a collection of product category documents, where each document corresponds to a node in the product ontology tree (1088 nodes total). Each document consists of sentences extracted from product descriptions which potentially describe its relationship to other product categories (based on the occurrence of category name labels). We can then use

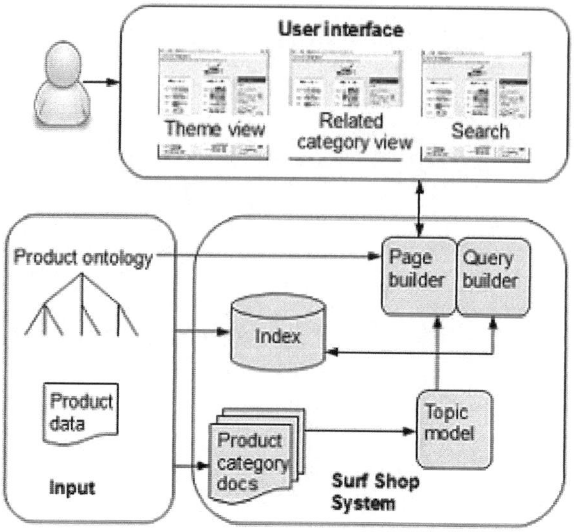

Figure 1: System overview

this artificially constructed corpus as input to LDA to discover hidden topics in the collection[4].

The topic model results, as well as product ontology information are combined with product search in order to build pages for our *SurfShop* application. In the prototype the user can move between search, browsing related categories, as well as browsing thematic product groupings. In the search mode, we use the query and the top n search results to infer which product category is most relevant to the query. This allows us to display links to related category groups next to the search results.

Given a product category, the users can also explore a related category map, such as the one shown in Figure 2 for *cheese*. They can browse example products in each related category by clicking on the category to load product information into the right column on the page. To provide example products, a query is issued under the relevant ontology node using the product category label and topic keywords, to ensure that we display items relevant to the current page. The product browsing functionality is similar for theme pages which are discussed in the next section.

[2]For an example see http://www.sccs.swarthmore.edu/users/08/ajb/tmve/wiki100k/browse/topic-list.html.

[3]We used an Apache Solr index and a JavaScript Ajax-Solr library from https://github.com/evolvingweb/ajax-solr.

[4]For LDA we used the Lingpipe package (http://alias-i.com/lingpipe/).

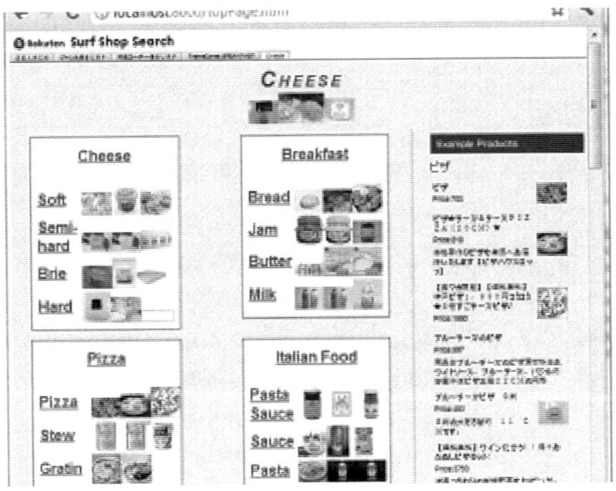

Figure 2: Related category page example. Category and theme labels have been translated into English.

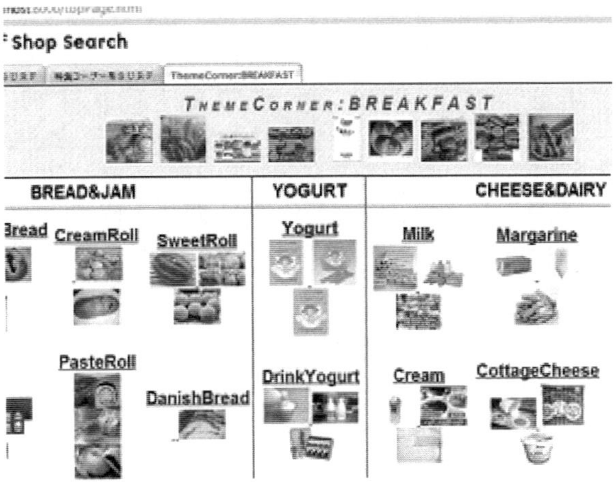

Figure 3: Theme page fragment. Category and theme labels have been translated into English.

3 Theme pages

An example of a *breakfast* theme page view is shown in Figure 3. It includes clusters of product categories which exemplify the page theme, such as *bread and jam* or *cheese and dairy*. Each theme page corresponds to a hidden topic discovered by the LDA model[5]. Human interpretation of topic models has been a focus of some recent work (Chang et al., 2009; Newman et al., 2010; Mimno et al., 2010). However, previous approaches concentrate on representing a topic by its top n most probable words. In contrast, our goal is to illustrate a topic by choosing the most representative documents from the collection, which also correspond to product categories associated with the topic. Since this is a novel task, we decided to concentrate on the issue of building and evaluating theme pages before conducting broader user studies of the prototype.

There are a few possible ways to select documents which best represent a topic. The simplest would be to consider the rank of this topic in the document. Alternatively, since the model provides an estimate of topic probability given a document, the probability that a product category document belongs to a topic could be calculated straightforwardly using the Bayes rule[6]. Yet another option for finding categories related to a given topic would be to assign a score based on KL divergence between the topic word multinomial and a product category multinomial, with the probability of each word w in the vocabulary defined as follows for a given category:

$$P(w) = \sum_{t}(P(w|t_i) * P(t_i|c_j)) \quad (1)$$

Finally, we hypothesized that product ontology structure may be helpful in creating the theme pages, since if one product category is representative of the topic, its sibling categories are also likely to be. Conversely, if a category is the only candidate for a given topic among its neighbors in the tree, it is less likely to be relevant. Therefore, we clustered the topic category candidates based on their distance in the ontology, and retained only the clusters with the highest average scores.

To evaluate which of the above methods is more effective, we gave the following task to a group of three Japanese annotators. For each topic we created a list of category candidates which included product categories where the topic ranked 1-3 (methods 1-3 in Table 1), top 25 Bayes score and KL divergence score categories (methods 4 and 5), as well as the categories based on ontology distance clusters combined with the Bayes score averages for cluster reliability (method 6). Each annotator was given a list of top ten keywords for each of the topics and asked to choose a suitable label based on the keywords. Subsequently, they were asked to select product cat-

[5]We empirically set the number of topics to 100. We removed top 10% most general topics, as defined by the number of documents which include the topic in its top 10.

[6]We made an additional simplifying assumption that all documents are equiprobable.

Scoring method	Precision	Recall	F-score
1.Rank1	73.83%	43.21%	54.16%
2.Rank1+2	50.91%	59.56%	54.54%
3.Rank1+2+3	41.71%	73.08%	52.77%
4.Top25 KL	53.54%	70.44%	60.45%
5.Top25 Bayes	53.56%	71.25%	60.76%
6.Bayes+Ont	66.71%	69.17%	67.48%

Table 1: Result average for three annotators on Task 1.

Scoring method	Precision	Recall	F-score
5.Top25 Bayes	71.28%	81.83%	76.03%
6.Bayes+Ont	84.11%	75.46%	79.38%

Table 2: Result average for three annotators on Task 2.

egories from the candidate list which fit the topic label they decided on.

In this manner, each annotator created their own "golden standard" of best categories which allowed us to compare the performance of different approaches to category selection. The amount of accepted categories varied, however a performance comparison of candidate sets showed consistent trends across annotators, which allows us to present averages over annotator scores in Table 1. Rank based selection increases in recall as lower ranks are included but the precision of the results decreases. KL divergence and Bayes rule based scores are comparable. Finally, combining the ontology information with Bayes scoring improves the precision, while retaining the recall similar to that of the top 25 Bayes score approach. We chose this last method to create theme pages.

We also wanted to verify how the presence of top topic words affects topic interpretation. In another task, shown in Table 2, the same group of annotators was presented only with product category lists which combined method 5 and method 6 candidates from the previous task. They were asked to assign a topic label which summarized the majority of those categories, as well as mark the categories which did not fit the topic. Even though the annotators had previously seen the same data, they tended to assign broader labels than those based on the top topic words, and included more categories as suitable for a given topic. For example, for the *breakfast* theme shown in Figure 3, one annotator labeled the topic *dairy products* based on topic words, and *bread and dairy products* based on the product category examples. The results of Task 2 led us to use manually assigned theme page labels based on the product category groupings rather than the topic keywords.

The differences in results between Task 1 and Task 2 indicate that, while top topic keywords aid interpretation, they may suggest a narrower theme than the documents selected to represent the topic and thus may not be optimal for some applications. This underscores the need for further research on human evaluation methods for topic models.

4 Future work

We demonstrated a prototype *SurfShop* system which employs product ontology structure and LDA model results to link associated product types and provide an entertaining browsing experience.

In the future we plan to replace the LDA component with a model which can directly account for the links found through the product ontology tree, such a version of the relational topic model (Chang and Blei, 2009). In addition, we hope that further exploration of theme page construction can contribute to the development of topic visualization and evaluation methods.

References

David M. Blei, Andrew Y. Ng, and Michael I. Jordan. 2003. Latent dirichlet allocation. *J. Mach. Learn.* Res. 3, 993-1022.

Jonathan Chang and David Blei. 2009. Relational topic models for document networks. *Proc. of Conf. on AI and Statistics*, 81-88.

J. Chang, J. Boyd-Graber, S. Gerrish, C. Wang, and D. Blei. 2009. Reading tea leaves: How humans interpret topic models. *NIPS*, 1-9.

David Mimno, Hanna Wallach, Edmund Talley, Miriam Leenders, and Andrew McCallum 2011. Optimizing semantic coherence in topic models. *EMNLP, 2011.*

David Newman, Jey Han Lau, Karl Grieser, and Timothy Baldwin. 2010. Automatic evaluation of topic coherence. *Human Language Technologies: The 2010 Annual Conference of the North American Chapter of the Association for Computational Linguistics*, 100-108.

An Interactive Humanoid Robot Exhibiting Flexible Sub-Dialogues*

Heriberto Cuayáhuitl
DFKI GmbH
hecu01@dfki.de

Ivana Kruijff-Korbayová
DFKI GmbH
ivana.kruijff@dfki.de

Abstract

We demonstrate a conversational humanoid robot that allows users to follow their own dialogue structures. Our system uses a hierarchy of reinforcement learning dialogue agents, which support transitions across sub-dialogues in order to relax the strictness of hierarchical control and therefore support flexible interactions. We demonstrate our system with the Nao robot playing two versions of a Quiz game. Whilst language input and dialogue control is autonomous or wizarded, language output is provided by the robot combining verbal and non-verbal contributions. The novel features in our system are (a) the flexibility given to users to navigate flexibly in the interaction; and (b) a framework for investigating adaptive and flexible dialogues.

1 Introduction

Hierarchical Dialogue Control (HDC) consists of behaviours or discourse segments at different levels of granularity executed from higher to lower level. For example, a dialogue agent can invoke a sub-dialogue agent, which can also invoke a sub-sub-dialogue agent, and so on. Task-oriented dialogues have shown evidence of following hierarchical structures (Grosz and Sidner, 1986; Litman and Allen, 1987; Clark, 1996). Practically speaking, HDC offers the following benefits. First, modularity helps to specify sub-dialogues that may be easier to specify than the entire full dialogues. Second, sub-dialogues may include only relevant dialogue knowledge (e.g. subsets of dialogue acts), thus reducing significantly their complexity. Third, sub-dialogues can be reused when dealing with new behaviours. In this paper we distinguish two types of hierarchical dialogue control: strict and flexible. These two forms of dialogue control are shown in Figure 1. It can be observed that strict HDC is based on a pure top down execution, and flexible HDC is based on a combined hierarchical and graph-based execution.

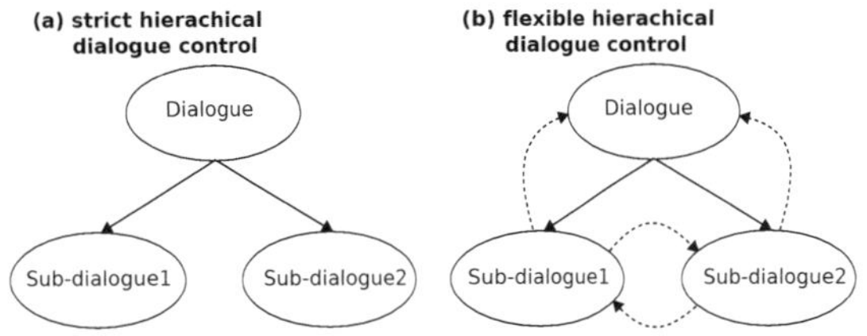

Figure 1: Hierarchies of dialogue agents with strict (top down) and flexible control (partial top down).

The main limitation of *strict* HDC is that human-machine interactions are rigid, i.e. the user cannot change the imposed dialogue structure. A more natural way of interaction is by relaxing the dialogue structure imposed by the conversational machine. The advantage of *flexible* HDC is that interactions become less rigid because it follows a partially specified hierarchical control, i.e. the user is allowed to navigate across the available sub-dialogues. In addition, another important property of the latter form of HDC is that we can model flexible dialogue structures not only driven by the user but also by the machine. The latter requires the machine to learn the dialogue structure in order to behave in an adaptive way. The rest of the paper describes a demo system exhibiting both types of behaviour, based on a reinforcement learning dialogue framework.

*Funding by the EU-FP7 project ALIZ-E (ICT-248116) is gratefully acknowledged.

Proceedings of the NAACL-HLT 2012: Demonstration Session, pages 17–20,
Montréal, Canada, June 3-8, 2012. ©2012 Association for Computational Linguistics

2 Hierarchical Reinforcement Learning Dialogue Agents with Flexible Control

Our dialogue controllers use hierarchical reinforcement learning as in (Cuayáhuitl et al., 2010). We extend such a formalization through a hierarchy of dialogue agents defined with the following tuples: $M^i_j = <S^i_j, A^i_j, T^i_j, R^i_j, L^i_j, U^i_j, \gamma^i_j, \delta^i_j>$, where S^i_j is a set of states, A^i_j is a set of actions, T^i_j is a stochastic state transition function, R^i_j is a reward function, L^i_j is a grammar that specifies tree-based state representations, U^i_j is a finite set of user actions (e.g. user dialogue acts), γ^i_j is a finite set of models that subtask M^i_j is being allowed to transition to, and $\delta^i_j = P(m' \in \gamma^i_j | m \in \gamma^i_j, u \in U^i_j)$ is a stochastic model transition function[1] that specifies the next model m' given model m and user action u. Although the hierarchy of agents can be fully-connected when all models are allowed to transition from a given particular model (avoiding self-transitions), in practice, we may want our hierarchy of agents partially-connected, i.e. when γ^i_j is a subset of subtasks that agent M^i_j is allowed to transition to.

We implemented a modified version of the *HSMQ-Learning* algorithm (Dietterich, 2000) to simultaneously learn a hierarchy of policies π^i_j. This algorithm uses a *stack* of subtasks and operates as illustrated in Figure 2. If during the execution of a subtask the user decides to jump to another subtask, i.e. to change to another sub-dialogue, the flexible execution of subtasks allows each subtask to be interrupted in two ways. In the first case, we check whether the new (active) subtask is already on the stack of subtasks to execute. This would be the case if it was a parent of the current subtask. In this case, we terminate execution of all intervening subtasks until we reach the parent subtask, which would be the new active subtask. Notice that termination of all intervening subtasks prevents the stack from growing infinitely. In the second case, the current subtask is put on hold, and if the new active subtask is not already on the stack of subtasks to execute, it is pushed onto the stack and control is passed to it. Once the new subtask terminates its execution, control is transferred back to the subtask on hold.

[1] This is a very relevant feature in dialogue agents in order to allow users to say and/or do anything at anytime, and the learning agents have to behave accordingly.

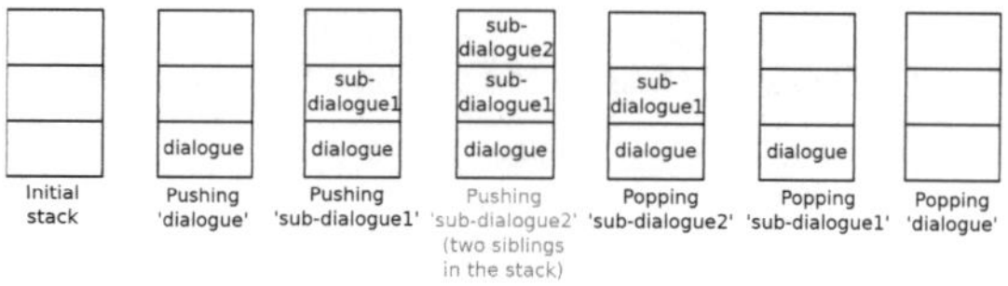

Figure 2: Hypothetical operations of stack-based hierarchical dialogue controllers. Whilst the fourth operation from left to right is not allowed in strict HDC, all stack operations are allowed in flexible HDC.

These kinds of transitions can be seen as high-level transitions in the state space. They can also be seen as the mechanism to transition from any state to any other in the hierarchy. To do that we maintain an activity status for each subtask M^i_j, where only one subtask is allowed to be active at a time. We maintain a knowledge-rich state that keeps the dialogue history in order to initialize or reinitialize states of each subtask accordingly. Since there is learning when new subtasks are invoked and no learning when they are interrupted, this algorithm maintains its convergence properties to optimal context-independent policies.

3 A Hierarchy of Dialogue Agents for Playing Quiz Games

We use a small hierarchy of dialogue agents—for illustration purposes—with one parent agent and two children agents ('robot asks' and 'user asks'). Thus, the hierarchy of agents can ask the user questions, and vice-versa, the user can ask the robot questions (described in the next section). Both conversants can play multiple rounds with a predefined number of questions.

Due to space restrictions, we describe the hierarchy of agents only briefly. The set of states and actions use relational representations (they can be seen as trees) in order to specify the state-action space compactly, which can grow as more features or games are integrated. Dialogue and game features are included so as to inform the agents of possible situations in the interaction. The action sets use constrained spaces, i.e. only a subset of actions is available at each state based on the relational representations. For example, the action $Request(PlayGame) \leftarrow x_0$ is valid for the dialogue state x_0 expressed as $Salutation(greeting) \wedge UserName(known) \wedge PlayGame(unknown)$. The sets of primitive actions (80 in total) assume verbal behaviours with a mapping to non-verbal ones, some sample dialogue act types are as follows: requests, apologies, confirmations, provide information, acknowledgements, feedback, non-verbal expressions, game-related actions. The transition functions use pre-defined parameters, their training from data is left as future work. The reward function addresses efficient and effective interactions by penalizing dialogue length and encouraging to continue playing. The dialogue agents learnt their behaviour by interacting with a stochastic simulated user, where the user responses eventually required transitions across agents. A sample dialogue with flexible interaction is shown in Fig. 3.

4 A Humanoid Robot Integrated System

Figure 4 shows the robot's integrated system, which equips the robot with the following capabilities: listening, talking, seeing and moving.[2] A sample interaction assuming wizarded behaviour is as follows. The user says something to the robot (e.g. 'ask me a question') and the wizard selects a user dialogue act for the corresponding utterance such as 'Request(Question)'. Then the dialogue manager selects and executes the learned action by querying/updating the game move generator and user model components, and by passing a dialogue act to the language generation and motor control components. The former provides the corresponding text to the speech synthesizer and the latter provides the corresponding non-verbal behaviour. Then the dialogue manager observes its new dialogue state, and suggests the next actions—based on its dialogue policies and user simulations—in the wizard-of-Oz GUI, see Figure 5. From this setting, if we remove the wizard then the system can behave autonomously, where user inputs are derived from the language and gesture understanding components.

The attractiveness of this kind of set-up is the smooth transition from purely wizarded conversational behaviour to fully autonomous behaviour, where the dialogue policies can be tested and eval-

[2]We use off-the-shelf technologies such as Sphinx / Julius / HTK for speech recognition, OpenCV for gesture recognition, Acapela and Mary for speech synthesis, HRL-based dialogue management (as described above), OpenCCG for language parsing and language generation, Weka and JavaBayes for maintaining a probabilistic and personalized user profile of asked and answered questions, the URBI middleware (`www.gostai.com`), and the NAO humanoid robot (`www.aldebaran-robotics.com`).

SYS	Hi, my name is NAO, and you?
USR	*I am Peter*
SYS	Nice to meet you Peter Do you want to Play a Quiz game?
USR	*Ask me questions [jump to 'robot asks']*
SYS	The first question is. What is a typical magic instrument? Your choices are: One, guitar. Two, drums. Three ,violin. Four, flute. What is your choice?
USR	*Number two*
SYS	That is not quite right. Do you have another choice?
USR	*Maybe number three*
SYS	The correct answer is number four, flute. The next question is: which one of these is an important artificial channel of the central America? Your choices are: One, channel five. Two, Panama canal. Three, Suez canal. Four, English channel. What is your choice?
USR	*Now I want to ask you questions [jump to 'user asks']*
SYS	Ask me the first question.
USR	*What does water become at the temperature of zero degrees?*
SYS	What are my choices?
USR	*Your choices are:* *One, condensation. Two, ice. Three, steam.*
SYS	I choose number one
USR	*That is incorrect.*
SYS	So what is the right answer?
USR	*The correct answer is number two.*
SYS	Okay, ask me another question.
USR	*The next question is: through which breach did* *the Italian army entered into Rome in 1870?* *Your choices are: One, porta venezia. Two, porta pia.* *Three, porta pazienza. Four, porta nuova.* *What is your choice?*
SYS	Paris
USR	*Let's stop playing. [jump to 'root']*
SYS	Did you like playing the Quiz Game?
USR	*Yes*
SYS	I am glad to hear that.
SYS	It was nice playing with you, see you soon. Bye!

Figure 3: Sample dialogue with non-strict hierarchical control. The groups of utterances represent activity in different sub-dialogues in the hierarchy of agents. Note that the user is allowed to override the imposed dialogue structure. For instance, when the user says 'Ask me questions' the agent interrupts the execution of the root subtask and transitions to the subtask 'robot asks'. Similarly, the sub-dialogues do not need to follow their imposed structure and the user is allowed to talk about previous and unadressed sub-dialogues such as the sudden switch from 'robot asks' to 'user asks'.

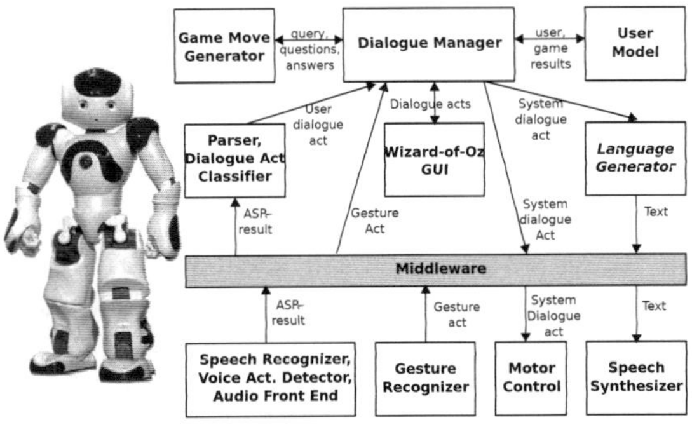

Figure 4: High-level architecture of our talking robot.

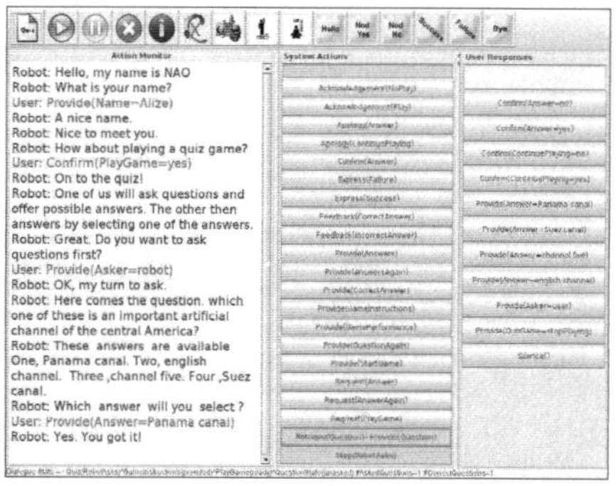

Figure 5: Screen shot of the wizard-of-Oz GUI, where the dialogue policies and user simulations suggest highlighted actions to the wizard. This setting allows fully-wizarded and (semi-) autonomous behaviour.

Figure 6: The Nao robot greeting a user prior to playing a Quiz game. The pieces of paper on the table are the Quiz questions the child asks the robot.

uated with (semi-) autonomous behaviour. We use this framework to investigate long-term human-robot interaction, in particular child-robot interactions for educational purposes. Figure 6 shows a scene from a pilot evaluation, where the robot and a child are visibly engaged with each other. A complete evaluation with simulated and real dialogues will be reported in a forthcoming paper.

5 Discussion and Summary

Typically, conversational interfaces impose a dialogue structure on the user. Even in dialogue systems with mixed-initiative interaction that give flexibility to the user in terms of providing more than one piece of information at a time, the user is hardly allowed to navigate flexibly during the interaction. Notable exceptions without dialogue optimization are (Rudnicky and Wu, 1999; Lemon et al., 2001; Larsson, 2002; Foster et al., 2006). We believe that Hierarchical Reinforcement Learning with global state transitions is an interesting method to optimize (sub-) dialogues at different levels of granularity, where the design of action selection might not be easy to hand-craft. On the one hand, our HDCs can be applied to dialogues with user-driven topic shift, where the user can take control of the interaction by navigating across sub-dialogues and the system has to respond accordingly. On the other hand, our HDCs can be applied to dialogues with system-driven topic shift, where the system can itself terminate a sub-dialogue, perhaps by inferring the user's emotional and/or situational state, and the system has to switch itself to another sub-dialogue.

We have described a conversational humanoid robot that allows users to follow their own dialogue structures. The novelty in our system is its flexible hierarchical dialogue controller, which extends strict hierarchical control with transitions across sub-controllers. Suggested future work consists in training and evaluating our humanoid robot from real interactions using either partially specified or fully learnt dialogue structures.

References

H. Clark. 1996. *Using Language*. Cambridge University Press.

H. Cuayáhuitl, S. Renals, O. Lemon, and H. Shimodaira. 2010. Evaluation of a hierarchical reinforcement learning spoken dialogue system. *Computer Speech and Language*, 24(2):395–429.

T. Dietterich. 2000. An overview of MAXQ hierarchical reinforcement learning. In *Symposium on Abstraction, Reformulation, and Approximation (SARA)*, pages 26–44.

M. E. Foster, T. By, M. Rickert, and A. Knoll. 2006. Human-robot dialogue for joint construction tasks. In *ICMI*, pages 68–71.

B. Grosz and C. Sidner. 1986. Attention, intentions and the structure of discourse. *Computational Linguistics*, 12(3):175–204.

S. Larsson. 2002. *Issue-Based Dialogue Management*. Ph.D. thesis, University of Goteborg.

O. Lemon, A. Bracy, A. Gruenstein, and S. Peters. 2001. The WITAS multi-modal dialogue system I. In *EUROSPEECH*, Aalborg, Denmark.

D. Litman and J. Allen. 1987. A plan recognition model for subdialogues in conversations. *Cognitive Science*, 11:163–200.

A. Rudnicky and W. Wu. 1999. An agenda-based dialogue management architecture for spoken language systems. In *IEEE Workshop on Automatic Speech Recognition and Understanding (ASRU)*, pages 337–340, Keystone, Colorado, USA, Dec.

MSR SPLAT, a language analysis toolkit

Chris Quirk, Pallavi Choudhury, Jianfeng Gao, Hisami Suzuki, Kristina Toutanova, Michael Gamon, Wen-tau Yih, Lucy Vanderwende
Microsoft Research
Redmond, WA 98052 USA

{chrisq, pallavic, jfgao, hisamis, kristout, mgamon,scottyih, lucyv@microsoft.com}

Colin Cherry

National Research Council Canada
1200 Montreal Road
Ottawa, Ontario K1A 0R6
colin.cherry@nrccnrc.gc.ca

Abstract

We describe MSR SPLAT, a toolkit for language analysis that allows easy access to the linguistic analysis tools produced by the NLP group at Microsoft Research. The tools include both traditional linguistic analysis tools such as part-of-speech taggers, constituency and dependency parsers, and more recent developments such as sentiment detection and linguistically valid morphology. As we expand the tools we develop for our own research, the set of tools available in MSR SPLAT will be extended. The toolkit is accessible as a web service, which can be used from a broad set of programming languages.

1 Introduction

The availability of annotated data sets that have become community standards, such as the Penn TreeBank (Marcus et al., 1993) and PropBank (Palmer et al., 2005), has enabled many research institutions to build core natural language processing components, including part-of-speech taggers, chunkers, and parsers. There remain many differences in how these components are built, resulting in slight but noticeable variation in the component output. In experimental settings, it has proved sometimes difficult to distinguish between improvements contributed by a specific component feature from improvements due to using a differently-trained linguistic component, such as tokenization. The community recognizes this difficulty, and shared task organizers are now providing accompanying parses and other analyses of the shared task data. For instance, the BioNLP shared task organizers have provided output from a number of parsers[1], alleviating the need for participating systems to download and run unfamiliar tools. On the other hand, many community members provide downloads of NLP tools[2] to increase accessibility and replicability of core components.

Our toolkit is offered in this same spirit. We have created well-tested, efficient linguistic tools in the course of our research, using commonly available resources such as the PTB and PropBank. We also have created some tools that are less commonly available in the community, for example linguistically valid base forms and semantic role analyzers. These components are on par with other state of the art systems.

We hope that sharing these tools will enable some researchers to carry out their projects without having to re-create or download commonly used NLP components, or potentially allow researchers to compare our results with those of their own tools. The further advantage of designing MSR SPLAT as a web service is that we can share new components on an on-going basis.

2 Parsing Functionality

2.1 Constituency Parsing

[1] See www-tsujii.is.s.u-tokyo.ac.jp/GENIA/SharedTask for the description of other resources made available in addition to the shared task data.

[2] See, for example, http://nlp.stanford.edu/software; http://www.informatics.sussex.ac.uk/research/groups/nlp/rasp; http://incubator.apache.org/opennlp

Proceedings of the NAACL-HLT 2012: Demonstration Session, pages 21–24,
Montréal, Canada, June 3-8, 2012.

The syntactic parser in MSR SPLAT attempts to reconstruct a parse tree according the Penn TreeBank specification (Marcus et al., 1993). This representation captures the notion of labeled syntactic constituents using a parenthesized representation. For instance, the sentence "Colorless green ideas sleep furiously." could be assigned the following parse tree, written in the form of an S expression:

```
(TOP (S
   (NP (JJ Colorless) (JJ green) (NNS ideas))
   (VP (VB sleep) (ADVP (RB furiously)))
   (. .)))
```

For instance, this parse tree indicates that "Colorless green ideas" is a noun phrase (NP), and "sleep furiously" is a verb phrase (VP).

Using the Wall Street Journal portion of the Penn TreeBank, we estimate a coarse grammar over the given grammar symbols. Next, we perform a series of refinements to automatically learn fine-grained categories that better capture the implicit correlations in the tree using the split-merge method of Petrov et al. (2006). Each input symbol is split into two new symbols, both with a new unique symbol label, and the grammar is updated to include a copy of each original rule for each such refinement, with a small amount of random noise added to the probability of each production to break ties. We estimate new grammar parameters using an accelerated form of the EM algorithm (Salakhutdinov and Roweis, 2003). Then the lowest 50% of the split symbols (according to their estimated contribution to the likelihood of the data) are merged back into their original form and the parameters are again re-estimated using AEM. We found six split-merge iterations produced optimal accuracy on the standard development set.

The best tree for a given input is selected according to the max-rule approach (cf. Petrov et al. 2006). Coarse-to-fine parsing with pruning at each level helps increase speed; pruning thresholds are picked for each level to have minimal impact on development set accuracy. However, the initial coarse pass still has runtime cubic in the length of the sentence. Thus, we limit the search space of the coarse parse by closing selected chart cells before the parse begins (Roark and Hollingshead, 2008). We train a classifier to determine if constituents may start or end at each position in the sentence. For instance, constituents seldom end at the word "the" or begin at a comma. Closing a number of chart cells can substantially improve runtime with minimal impact on accuracy.

2.2 Dependency Parsing

The dependency parses produced by MSR SPLAT are unlabeled, directed arcs indicating the syntactic governor of each word.

These dependency trees are computed from the output of the constituency parser. First, the head of each non-terminal is computed according to a set of rules (Collins, 1999). Then, the tree is flattened into maximal projections of heads. Finally, we introduce an arc from a parent word p to a child word c if the non-terminal headed by p is a parent of the non-terminal headed by c.

2.3 Semantic Role Labeling

The Semantic Role Labeling component of MSR SPLAT labels the semantic roles of verbs according to the PropBank specification (Palmer et al., 2005). The semantic roles represent a level of broad-coverage shallow semantic analysis which goes beyond syntax, but does not handle phenomena like co-reference and quantification.

For example, in the two sentences "John broke the window" and "The window broke", the phrase *the window* will be marked with a THEME label. Note that the syntactic role of the phrase in the two sentences is different but the semantic role is the same. The actual labeling scheme makes use of numbered argument labels, like ARG0, ARG1, …, ARG5 for core arguments, and labels like ARGM-TMP,ARGM-LOC, etc. for adjunct-like arguments. The meaning of the numbered arguments is verb-specific, with ARG0 typically representing an agent-like role, and ARG1 a patient-like role.

This implementation of an SRL system follows the approach described in (Xue and Palmer, 04), and includes two log-linear models for argument identification and classification. A single syntax tree generated by the MSR SPLAT split-merge parser is used as input. Non-overlapping arguments are derived using the dynamic programming algorithm by Toutanova et al. (2008).

3 Other Language Analysis Functionality

3.1 Sentence Boundary / Tokenization

This analyzer identifies sentence boundaries and breaks the input into tokens. Both are represented as offsets of character ranges. Each token has both a raw form from the string and a normalized form in the PTB specification, e.g., open and close parentheses are replaced by -LRB- and -RRB-, respectively, to remove ambiguity with parentheses indicating syntactic structure. A finite state machine using simple rules and abbreviations detects sentence boundaries with high accuracy, and a set of regular expressions tokenize the input.

3.2 Stemming / Lemmatization

We provide three types of stemming: Porter stemming, inflectional morphology and derivational morphology.

3.2.1 Stems

The stemmer analyzer indicates a stem form for each input token, using the standard Porter stemming algorithm (Porter, 1980). These forms are known to be useful in applications such as clustering, as the algorithm assigns the same form "dai" to "daily" and "day", but as these forms are not citation forms of these words, presentation to end users is known to be problematic.

3.2.2 Lemmas

The lemma analyzer uses inflectional morphology to indicate the dictionary lookup form of the word. For example, the lemma of "daily" will be "daily", while the lemma of "children" will be "child". We have mined the lemma form of input tokens using a broad-coverage grammar NLPwin (Heidorn, 2000) over very large corpora.

3.2.3 Bases

The base analyzer uses derivational morphology to indicate the dictionary lookup form of the word; as there can be more than one derivation for a given word, the base type returns a list of forms. For example, the base form of "daily" will be "day", while the base form of "additional" will be "addition" and "add". We have generated a static list of base forms of tokens using a broad-coverage grammar NLPwin (Heidorn, 2000) over very large corpora. If the token form has not been observed in those corpora, we will not return a base form.

3.3 POS tagging

We train a maximum entropy Markov Model on part-of-speech tags from the Penn TreeBank. This optimized implementation has very high accuracy (over 96% on the test set) and yet can tag tens of thousands of words per second.

3.4 Chunking

The chunker (Gao et al., 2001) is based on a Cascaded Markov Model, and is trained on the Penn TreeBank. With state-of-the-art chunking accuracy as evaluated on the benchmark dataset, the chunker is also robust and efficient, and has been used to process very large corpora of web documents.

4 The Flexibility of a Web Service

By making the MSR SPLAT toolkit available as a web service, we can provide access to new tools, e.g. sentiment analysis. We are in the process of building out the tools to provide language analysis for languages other than English. One step in this direction is a tool for transliterating between English and Katakana words. Following Cherry and Suzuki (2009), the toolkit currently outputs the 10-best transliteration candidates with probabilities for both directions.

Another included service is the Triples analyzer, which returns the head of the subject, the verb, and the head of the object, whenever such a triple is encountered. We found this functionality to be useful as we were exploring features for our system submitted to the BioNLP shared task.

5 Programmatic Access

5.1 Web service reference

We have designed a web service that accepts a batch of text and applies a series of analysis tools to that text, returning a bag of analyses. This main web service call, named "Analyze", requires four parameters: the language of the text (such as "en" for English), the raw text to be analyzed, the set of analyzers to apply, and an access key to monitor and, if necessary, constrain usage. It returns a list of analyses, one from each requested analyzer, in a

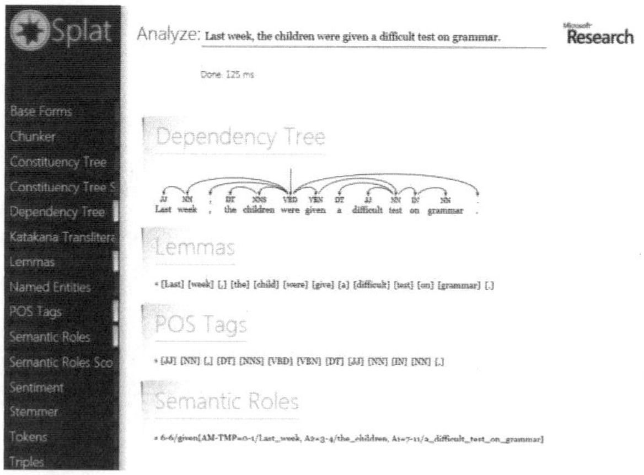

Figure 1. Screenshot of the MSR SPLAT interactive UI showing selected functionalities which can be toggled on and off. This is the interface that we propose to demo at NAACL.

simple JSON (JavaScript Object Notation) format easy to parse in many programming languages.

In addition, there is a web service call "Languages" that enumerates the list of available languages, and "Analyzers" to discover the set of analyzers available in a given language.

5.2 Data Formats

We use a relatively standard set of data representations for each component. Parse trees are returned as S expressions, part-of-speech tags are returned as lists, dependency trees are returned as lists of parent indices, and so on. The website contains an authoritative description of each analysis format.

5.3 Speed

Speed of analysis is heavily dependent on the component involved. Analyzers for sentence separation, tokenization, and part-of-speech tagging process thousands of sentences per second; our fastest constituency parser handles tens of sentences per second. Where possible, the user is encouraged to send moderate sized requests (perhaps a paragraph at a time) to minimize the impact of network latency.

6 Conclusion

We hope that others will find the tools that we have made available as useful as we have. We encourage people to send us their feedback so that we can improve our tools and increase collaboration in the community.

7 Script Outline

The interactive UI (Figure 1) allows an arbitrary sentence to be entered and the desired levels of analysis to be selected as output. As there exist other such toolkits, the demonstration is primarily aimed at allowing participants to assess the quality, utility and speed of the MSR SPLAT tools. http://research.microsoft.com/en-us/projects/msrsplat/

References

Colin Cherry and Hisami Suzuki. 2009. Discriminative substring decoding for transliteration. In *Proceedings of EMNLP.*

Michael Collins. 1999. *Head-driven statistical models for natural language parsing.* PhD Dissertation, University of Pennsylvania.

Jianfeng Gao, Jian-Yun Nie, Jian Zhang, Endong Xun, Ming Zhou and Chang-Ning Huang. 2001. Improving query translation for CLIR using statistical Models. *In Proceedings of SIGIR.*

George Heidorn. 2000. Intelligent writing assistance. In R. Dale, H. Moisl and H. Somers (eds.), *A Handbook of Natural Language Processing: Techniques and Applications for the Processing of Text.* New York: Marcel Dekker.

Mitchell Marcus, Beatrice Santorini, and Mary Ann Marcinkiewicz. 1993. Building a Large Annotated Corpus of English: The Penn Treebank. *Computational Linguistics* 19(2): 313-330.

Martha Palmer, Dan Gildea, Paul Kingsbury. 2005. The Proposition Bank: An Annotated Corpus of Semantic Roles. *Computational Linguistics*, 31(1): 71-105

Martin Porter. 1980. An algorithm for suffix stripping. *Program*, 14(3): 130-137.

Slav Petrov, Leon Barrett, Romain Thibaux, and Dan Klein. 2006. Learning Accurate, Compact, and Interpretable Tree Annotation. In *Proceedings of ACL.*

Brian Roark and Kristy Hollingshead. 2008. Classifying chart cells for quadratic complexity context-free inference. In *Proceedings of COLING.*

Ruslan Salakhutdinov and Sam Roweis. 2003. Adaptive Overrelaxed Bound Optimization Methods. In *Proceedings of ICML.*

Kristina Toutanova, Aria Haghighi, and Christopher D. Manning. 2008. A global joint model for semantic role labeling, *Computational Linguistics*, 34(2): 161-191.

Nianwen Xue and Martha Palmer. 2004. Calibrating Features for Semantic Role Labeling. In *Proceedings of EMNLP.*

Munmun de Choudhury, Scott Counts, Michael Gamon. Not All Moods are Created Equal! Exploring Human Emotional States in Social Media. Accepted for presentation in *ICWSM 2012*

Munmun de Choudhury, Scott Counts, Michael Gamon. Happy, Nervous, Surprised? Classification of Human Affective States in Social Media. Accepted for presentation (short paper) in *ICWSM 2012*

Incremental Speech Understanding in a Multi-Party Virtual Human Dialogue System

David DeVault and **David Traum**
Institute for Creative Technologies
University of Southern California
12015 Waterfront Drive, Playa Vista, CA 90094
{devault,traum}@ict.usc.edu

1 Extended Abstract

This demonstration highlights some emerging capabilities for incremental speech understanding and processing in virtual human dialogue systems. This work is part of an ongoing effort that aims to enable realistic spoken dialogue with virtual humans in multi-party negotiation scenarios (Plüss et al., 2011; Traum et al., 2008b). These scenarios are designed to allow trainees to practice their negotiation skills by engaging in face-to-face spoken negotiation with one or more virtual humans.

An important component in achieving naturalistic behavior in these negotiation scenarios, which ideally should have the virtual humans demonstrating fluid turn-taking, complex reasoning, and responding to factors like trust and emotions, is for the virtual humans to begin to understand and in some cases respond in real time to users' speech, as the users are speaking (DeVault et al., 2011b). These responses could range from relatively straightforward turn management behaviors, like having a virtual human recognize when it is being addressed by a user utterance, and possibly turn to look at the user who has started speaking, to more complex responses such as emotional reactions to the content of what users are saying.

The current demonstration extends our previous demonstration of incremental processing (Sagae et al., 2010) in several important respects. First, it includes additional indicators, as described in (DeVault et al., 2011a). Second, it is applied to a new domain, an extension of that presented in (Plüss et al., 2011). Finally, it is integrated with the dialogue

Figure 1: SASO negotiation in the saloon: Utah (left) looking at Harmony (right).

models (Traum et al., 2008a), such that each partial interpretation is given a full pragmatic interpretation by each virtual character, which can be used to generate real-time incremental non-verbal feedback (Wang et al., 2011).

Our demonstration is set in an implemented multi-party negotiation domain (Plüss et al., 2011) in which two virtual humans, Utah and Harmony (pictured in Figure 1), talk with two human negotiation trainees, who play the roles of Ranger and Deputy. The dialogue takes place inside a saloon in an American town in the Old West. In this negotiation scenario, the goal of the two human role players is to convince Utah and Harmony that Utah, who is currently employed as the local bartender, should take on the job of town sheriff.

One of the research aims for this work is to support natural dialogue interaction, an example of which is the excerpt of human role play dialogue shown in Figure 2. One of the key features of immersive role plays is that people often react in multiple ways to the utterances of others as they are speaking. For example, in this excerpt, the beginning of the

Proceedings of the NAACL-HLT 2012: Demonstration Session, pages 25–28,
Montréal, Canada, June 3-8, 2012. ©2012 Association for Computational Linguistics

Ranger	We can't leave this place and have it overrun by outlaws. Uh there's no way that's gonna happen so we're gonna make sure we've got a properly deputized and equipped sheriff ready to maintain order in this area. *00:03:56.660 - 00:04:08.830*
Deputy	Yeah and you know and and we're willing to *00:04:06.370 - 00:04:09.850*
Utah	And I don't have to leave the bar completely. I can still uh be here part time and I can um we can hire someone to do the like day to day work and I'll do the I'll supervise them and I'll teach them. *00:04:09.090 - 00:04:22.880*

Figure 2: Dialogue excerpt from one of the role plays. Timestamps indicate the start and end of each utterance.

Deputy's utterance overlaps the end of the Ranger's, and then Utah interrupts the Deputy and takes the floor a few seconds later.

Our prediction approach to incremental speech understanding utilizes a corpus of in-domain spoken utterances, including both paraphrases selected and spoken by system developers, as well as spoken utterances from user testing sessions (DeVault et al., 2011b). An example of a corpus element is shown in Figure 3. In previous negotiation domains, we have found a fairly high word error rate in automatic speech recognition results for such spontaneous multi-party dialogue data; for example, our average word error rate was 0.39 in the SASO-EN negotiation domain (Traum et al., 2008b) with many (15%) out of domain utterances. Our speech understanding framework is robust to these kinds of problems (DeVault et al., 2011b), partly through approximating the meaning of utterances. Utterance meanings are represented using an attribute-value matrix (AVM), where the attributes and values represent semantic information that is linked to a domain-specific ontology and task model (Traum, 2003; Hartholt et al., 2008; Plüss et al., 2011). The AVMs are linearized, using a path-value notation, as seen in Figure 3. In our framework, we use this data to train two data-driven models, one for incremental natural language understanding, and a second for incremental confidence modeling.

The first step is to train a predictive incremental understanding model. This model is based on maximum entropy classification, and treats entire individual frames as output classes, with input features extracted from partial ASR results, calculated in increments of 200 milliseconds (DeVault et al., 2011b).

- Utterance (speech): *i've come here today to talk to you about whether you'd like to become the sheriff of this town*
- ASR (NLU input): *have come here today to talk to you about would the like to become the sheriff of this town*
- Frame (NLU output):

```
<S>.mood interrogative
<S>.sem.modal.desire want
<S>.sem.prop.agent utah
<S>.sem.prop.event providePublicServices
<S>.sem.prop.location town
<S>.sem.prop.theme sheriff-job
<S>.sem.prop.type event
<S>.sem.q-slot polarity
<S>.sem.speechact.type info-req
<S>.sem.type question
```

Figure 3: Example of a corpus training example.

Each partial ASR result then serves as an incremental input to NLU, which is specially trained for partial input as discussed in (Sagae et al., 2009). NLU is predictive in the sense that, for each partial ASR result, the NLU module produces as output the *complete* frame that has been associated by a human annotator with the user's *complete* utterance, even if that utterance has not yet been fully processed by the ASR. For a detailed analysis of the performance of the predictive NLU, see (DeVault et al., 2011b).

The second step in our framework is to train a set of incremental confidence models (DeVault et al., 2011a), which allow the agents to assess in real time, while a user is speaking, how well the understanding process is proceeding. The incremental confidence models build on the notion of NLU F-score, which we use to quantify the quality of a predicted NLU frame in relation to the hand-annotated correct frame. The NLU F-score is the harmonic mean of the precision and recall of the attribute-value pairs (or *frame elements*) that compose the predicted and correct frames for each partial ASR result. By using precision and recall of frame elements, rather than simply looking at frame accuracy, we take into account that certain frames are more similar than others, and allow for cases when the correct frame is not in the training set.

Each of our incremental confidence models makes a binary prediction for each partial NLU result as an utterance proceeds. At each time t dur-

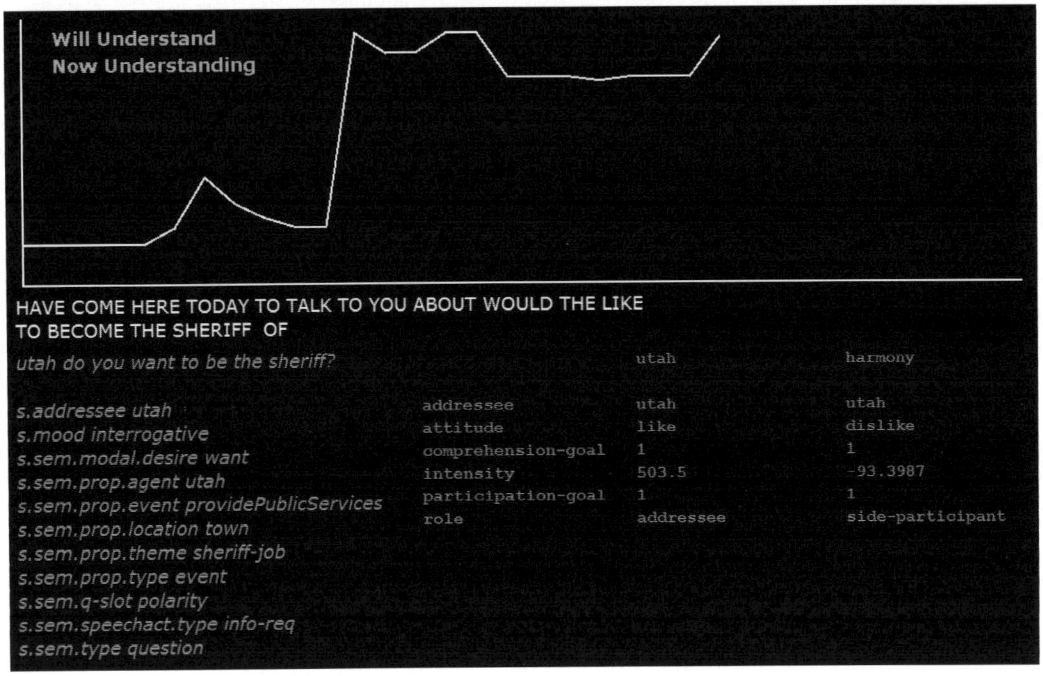

Figure 4: Visualization of Incremental Speech Processing.

ing an utterance, we consider the current NLU F-Score F_t as well as the final NLU F-Score F_{final} that will be achieved at the conclusion of the utterance. In (DeVault et al., 2009) and (DeVault et al., 2011a), we explored the use of data-driven decision tree classifiers to make predictions about these values, for example whether $F_t \geq \frac{1}{2}$ (current level of understanding is "high"), $F_t \geq F_{\text{final}}$ (current level of understanding will not improve), or $F_{\text{final}} \geq \frac{1}{2}$ (final level of understanding will be "high"). In this demonstration, we focus on the first and third of these incremental confidence metrics, which we summarize as "Now Understanding" and "Will Understand", respectively. In an evaluation over all partial ASR results for 990 utterances in this new scenario, we found the Now Understanding model to have precision/recall/F-Score of .92/.75/.82, and the Will Understand model to have precision/recall/F-Score of .93/.85/.89. These incremental confidence models therefore provide potentially useful real-time information to Utah and Harmony about whether they are currently understanding a user utterance, and whether they will ever understand a user utterance.

The incremental ASR, NLU, and confidence models are passed to the dialogue managers for each of the agents, Harmony and Utah. These agents then relate these inputs to their own models of dialogue context, plans, and emotions, to calculate pragmatic interpretations, including speech acts, reference resolution, participant status, and how they feel about what is being discussed. A subset of this information is passed to the non-verbal behavior generation module to produce incremental non-verbal listening behaviors (Wang et al., 2011).

In support of this demonstration, we have extended the implementation to include a real-time visualization of incremental speech processing results, which will allow attendees to track the virtual humans' understanding as an utterance progresses. An example of this visualization is shown in Figure 4.

2 Demo script

The demonstration begins with the demo operator providing a brief overview of the system design, negotiation scenario, and incremental processing capabilities. The virtual humans Utah and Harmony (see Figure 1) are running and ready to begin a dialogue with the user, who will play the role of the Ranger. As the user speaks to Utah or Harmony, attendees can observe the real time visualization of speech processing to observe changes in the incremental processing results as the utterance progresses. Further, the visualization interface enables the demo operator to "rewind" an utterance and step through the incremental processing results that arrived each 200 milliseconds, highlighting how specific partial ASR results can change the virtual humans' understanding or confidence.

For example, Figure 4 shows the incremental speech processing state at a moment 4.8 seconds into a user's 7.4 second long utterance, *i've come here today to talk to you about whether you'd like to become the sheriff of this town.* At this point in time, the visualization shows (at top left) that the virtual humans are confident that they are both Now Understanding and Will Understand this utterance. Next, the graph (in white) shows the history of the agents' expected NLU F-Score for this utterance (ranging from 0 to 1). Beneath the graph, the partial ASR result (`HAVE COME HERE TODAY TO TALK TO YOU ABOUT...`) is displayed (in white), along with the currently predicted NLU frame (in blue). For ease of comprehension, an English gloss (*utah do you want to be the sheriff?*) for the NLU frame is also shown (in blue) above the frame.

To the right, in pink, we show some of Utah and Harmony's agent state that is based on the current incremental NLU results. The display shows that both of the virtual humans believe that Utah is being addressed by this utterance, that utah has a positive attitude toward the content of the utterance while harmony does not, and that both have comprehension and participation goals. Further, Harmony believes she is a side participant at this moment. The demo operator will explain and discuss this agent state information, including possible uses for this information in response policies.

Acknowledgments

We thank all the members of the ICT Virtual Humans team. The project or effort described here has been sponsored by the U.S. Army Research, Development, and Engineering Command (RDECOM). Statements and opinions expressed do not necessarily reflect the position or the policy of the United States Government, and no official endorsement should be inferred.

References

David DeVault, Kenji Sagae, and David Traum. 2009. Can I finish? Learning when to respond to incremental interpretation results in interactive dialogue. In *Proceedings of SIGDIAL*.

David DeVault, Kenji Sagae, and David Traum. 2011a. Detecting the status of a predictive incremental speech understanding model for real-time decision-making in a spoken dialogue system. In *Proceedings of InterSpeech*.

David DeVault, Kenji Sagae, and David Traum. 2011b. Incremental interpretation and prediction of utterance meaning for interactive dialogue. *Dialogue & Discourse*, 2(1).

Arno Hartholt, Thomas Russ, David Traum, Eduard Hovy, and Susan Robinson. 2008. A common ground for virtual humans: Using an ontology in a natural language oriented virtual human architecture. In *Proceedings of LREC*, Marrakech, Morocco, may.

Brian Plüss, David DeVault, and David Traum. 2011. Toward rapid development of multi-party virtual human negotiation scenarios. In *Proceedings of SemDial 2011, the 15th Workshop on the Semantics and Pragmatics of Dialogue*.

Kenji Sagae, Gwen Christian, David DeVault, and David R. Traum. 2009. Towards natural language understanding of partial speech recognition results in dialogue systems. In *Short Paper Proceedings of NAACL HLT*.

Kenji Sagae, David DeVault, and David R. Traum. 2010. Interpretation of partial utterances in virtual human dialogue systems. In *Demonstration Proceedings of NAACL-HLT*.

D. Traum, W. Swartout, J. Gratch, and S. Marsella. 2008a. A virtual human dialogue model for non-team interaction. In L. Dybkjaer and W. Minker, editors, *Recent Trends in Discourse and Dialogue*. Springer.

David Traum, Stacy Marsella, Jonathan Gratch, Jina Lee, and Arno Hartholt. 2008b. Multi-party, multi-issue, multi-strategy negotiation for multi-modal virtual agents. In *Proceedings of IVA*.

David Traum. 2003. Semantics and pragmatics of questions and answers for dialogue agents. In *Proc. of the International Workshop on Computational Semantics*, pages 380–394, January.

Zhiyang Wang, Jina Lee, and Stacy Marsella. 2011. Towards more comprehensive listening behavior: Beyond the bobble head. In Hannes Vilhjlmsson, Stefan Kopp, Stacy Marsella, and Kristinn Thrisson, editors, *Intelligent Virtual Agents*, volume 6895 of *Lecture Notes in Computer Science*, pages 216–227. Springer Berlin / Heidelberg.

A Robust Shallow Temporal Reasoning System

Ran Zhao **Quang Xuan Do** **Dan Roth**
Computer Science Department
University of Illinois at Urbana-Champaign
Urbana, IL 61801, USA
{ranzhao1,quangdo2,danr}@illinois.edu

Abstract

This paper presents a demonstration of a temporal reasoning system that addresses three fundamental tasks related to temporal expressions in text: extraction, normalization to time intervals and comparison. Our system makes use of an existing state-of-the-art temporal extraction system, on top of which we add several important novel contributions. In addition, we demonstrate that our system can perform temporal reasoning by comparing normalized temporal expressions with respect to several temporal relations. Experimental study shows that the system achieves excellent performance on all the tasks we address.

1 Introduction

Performing temporal reasoning with respect to temporal expressions is important in many NLP tasks such as text summarization, information extraction, discourse understanding and information retrieval. Recently, the Knowledge Base Population track (Ji et al., 2011) introduced the temporal slot filling task that requires identifying and extracting temporal information for a limited set of binary relations such as (*person*, *employee_of*), (*person*, *spouse*). In the work of (Wang et al., 2010), the authors presented the Timely Yago ontology, which extracted and incorporated temporal information as part of the description of the events and relations in the ontology. Temporal reasoning is also essential in supporting the emerging temporal information retrieval research direction (Alonso et al., 2011).

In this paper, we present a system that addresses three fundamental tasks in temporal reasoning:

- *Extraction*: Capturing the extent of time expressions in a given text. This task is based on task A in the TempEval-2 challenge (Verhagen et al., 2010). Consider the following sentence:

  Seventy-five million copies of the rifle have been built since it entered production in February 1947.

  In this sentence, *February 1947* is a basic temporal expression that should be extracted by the extraction module. More importantly, we further extend the task to support also the extraction of *complex temporal expressions* that are not addressed by existing systems. In the example above, it is important to recognize and capture the phrase *since it entered production in February 1947* as another temporal expression that expresses the time period of the *manufacturing* event (triggered by *built*.) For the best of our knowledge, this extension is novel.
- *Normalization*: Normalizing temporal expressions, which are extracted by the extraction module, to a canonical form. Our system normalizes temporal expressions (including complex ones) to time intervals of the form [*start point*, *end point*]. The endpoints follow a standard date and time format: *YYYY-MM-DD hh:mm:ss*. Our system accounts for an input reference date when performing the normalization. For example, given March 20th, 1947 as a reference date, our system normalizes the temporal expressions extracted in the example above as follows: [*1947-02-01 00:00:00*, *1947-02-28 23:59:59*] and [*1947-02-01 00:00:00*, *1947-03-20 23:59:59*], respectively.
- *Comparison*: Comparing two time intervals (i.e. normalized temporal expressions). This module identifies the temporal relation that holds be-

Proceedings of the NAACL-HLT 2012: Demonstration Session, pages 29–32,
Montréal, Canada, June 3-8, 2012.

tween intervals, including the *before*, *before-and-overlap*, *containing*, *equal*, *inside* , *after* and *after-and-overlap* relations. For example, when comparing the two normalized time intervals above, we get the following result: [*1947-02-01 00:00:00, 1947-02-28 23:59:59*] is *inside* [*1947-02-01 00:00:00, 1947-03-20 23:59:59*].

There has been much work addressing the problems of temporal expression extraction and normalization, i.e. the systems developed in TempEval-2 challenge (Verhagen et al., 2010). However, our system is different from them in several aspects. First, we extend the extraction task to capture complex temporal expressions. Second, our system normalizes temporal expressions (including complex ones) to time intervals instead of time points. Finally, our system performs temporal comparison of time intervals with respect to multiple relations. We believe that with the rapid progress in NLP and IR, more tasks will require temporal information and reasoning, and a system that addresses these three fundamental tasks well will be able to support and facilitate temporal reasoning systems efficiently.

2 The System

2.1 Temporal Expression Extraction

We built the temporal expression extraction module on top of the Heideltime system (Strötgen and Gertz, 2010) to take advantage of a state-of-the-art temporal extraction system in capturing basic expressions. We use the Illinois POS tagger[1] (Roth and Zelenko, 1998) to provide part-of-speech tags for the input text before passing it to HeidelTime. Below is an example of the HeidelTime output of the example in the previous section:

> Seventy-five million copies of the rifle have been built since it entered production in <TIMEX3 tid="t2" type="DATE" value="1947-02">February 1947</TIMEX3>

In this example, HeidelTime captures a basic temporal expression: *February 1947*. However, HeidelTime cannot capture the complex temporal expression *since it entered production in February 1947*, which expresses a period of time from February 1947 until the document creation time. This is actually the time period of the manufacturing event (triggered by *built*). To capture complex phrases, we make use of a syntactic parse tree[2] as illustrated in Figure 1. A complex temporal expression is recognized if it satisfies the following conditions:

- It is covered by a PP or SBAR constituent in the parse tree.
- The constituent starts with a temporal connective. In this work, we focus on an important subset of temporal connectives, consisting of *since*, *between*, *from*, *before* and *after*.
- It contains at least one basic temporal expression extracted by HeidelTime.

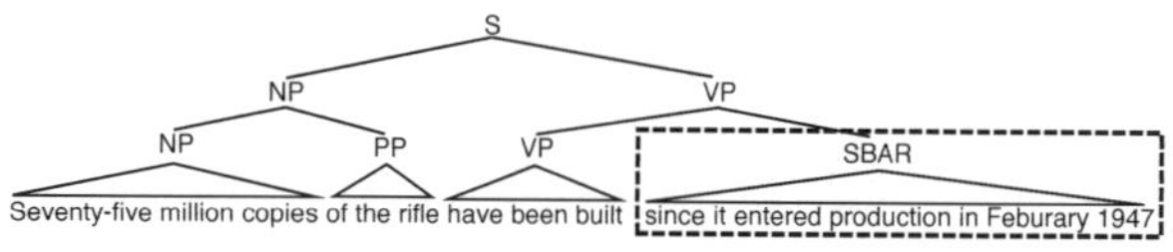

Figure 1: The SBAR constituent in the parse tree determines an extended temporal expression given that *in February 1947* is already captured by HeidelTime.

In addition, our extraction module also handles holidays in several countries. For example, in the sentence "The gas price increased rapidly after Christmas.", we are able to extract two temporal expressions *Christmas* and *after Christmas*, which refer to different time intervals.

2.2 Normalization to Time Intervals

Our system normalizes a temporal expression to a time interval of the form [*start point*, *end point*], where *start point* $\leq$ *end point*. Each time endpoint of an interval follows a standard date and time format: *YYYY-MM-DD hh:mm:ss*. It is worth noting that this format augments the date format in TimeML, used by HeidelTime and other existing systems. Our date and time format of each time endpoint refer to an absolute time point on a universal timeline, making our time intervals absolute as well. Furthermore, we take advantage of the predicted temporal value of each temporal expression from the HeidelTime output. For instance, in the HeidelTime output example above, we extract *1947-02* as the normalized date of *February 1947* and then convert it to the interval [*1947-02-01 00:00:00, 1947-02-28 23:59:59*]. If HeidelTime cannot identify an exact date, month or year, we then resort to our own temporal normalizer,

[1] http://cogcomp.cs.illinois.edu/page/software_view/POS

[2] We use nlparser (Charniak and Johnson, 2005)

which consists of a set of conversion rules, regarding to the document creation time of the input text. An interval endpoint can get infinity value if its temporal boundary cannot be specified.

2.3 Comparison

To compare two time intervals (i.e. normalized temporal expressions), we define six temporal relations: *before*, *before-and-overlap*, *contains*, *equals*, *inside*, *after* and *after-and-overlap*. The temporal relation between two normalized intervals is determined by a set of comparison rules that take the four interval endpoints into consideration. For example, $A = [s_A, e_A]$ *contains* $B = [s_B, e_B]$ if and only if $(s_A < s_B) \wedge (e_A > e_B)$, where s and e are intervals start and end points, respectively.

3 Experimental Study

In this section, we present an evaluation of our extended temporal extractor, the normalizer and the comparator. We do not evaluate the HeidelTime temporal extractor again because its performance was reported in the TempEval-2 challenge (Verhagen et al., 2010), where it achieved 0.86 F_1 score on the TimeBank data sets (Pustejovsky et al., 2003).

3.1 Data Preparation

We focus on scaling up temporal systems to deal with complex expressions. Therefore, we prepared an evaluation data set that consists of a list of sentences containing at least one of the five temporal connectives *since*, *betwen*, *from*, *before* and *after*. To do this, we extract all sentences that satisfy the condition from 183 articles in the TimeBank 1.2 corpus[3]. This results in a total of 486 sentences. Each sentence in the data set comes with the document creation time (DCT) of its corresponding article. The second and the third columns of Table 1 summarize the number of sentences and appearances of each temporal connective.

We use this data set to evaluate the extended temporal extractor, the normalizer and also the comparator of our system. We note that although this data set is driven by our focused temporal connectives, it does not lose the generality of evaluating

[3]http://www.ldc.upenn.edu/Catalog/catalogEntry.jsp?catalogId=LDC2006T08

Connective	# sent.	# appear.	Prec	Rec	F_1
since	31	31	1.0	1.0	1.0
between	32	33	1.0	1.0	1.0
from	340	366	0.8	1.0	0.89
before	33	33	0.8	1.0	0.89
after	78	81	0.72	1.0	0.84
Avg.			0.86	1.0	0.92

Table 1: The performance of our extended temporal extractor on complex expressions which contain at least one of the connectives shown in the first column. These expressions cannot be identified by existing systems.

Module	Correct	Incorrect	Acc
Normalizer	191	16	0.92
Comparator	191	0	1.0

Table 2: The performance of the normalization and comparison modules. We only compare the 191 correctly identified time intervals with their corresponding document creation time.

the normalization and comparison modules because the sentences in this data set also contain many basic temporal expressions. Moreover, there are many cases where the connectives in our data are not actually temporal connectives. Our system is supposed to not capture them as temporal expressions. This is also reflected in the experimental results.

3.2 Experimental Results

We report the performance of our extended temporal extraction module using precision, recall and F_1 score as shown in the last three columns of Table 1. We evaluate the normalization module on the correctly extracted temporal expressions, including basic expressions captured by HeidelTime and the extended expressions identified by our extractor. A normalization is correct if and only if both time interval endpoints are correctly identified. We study the comparison module by evaluating it on the comparisons of the correctly normalized expressions against the corresponding DCT of the sentences from which they are extracted. Because the normalization and comparison outputs are judged as correct or incorrect, we report the performance of these modules in accuracy (Acc) as shown in Table 2. Overall, the experimental study shows that all modules in our system are robust and achieve excellent performance.

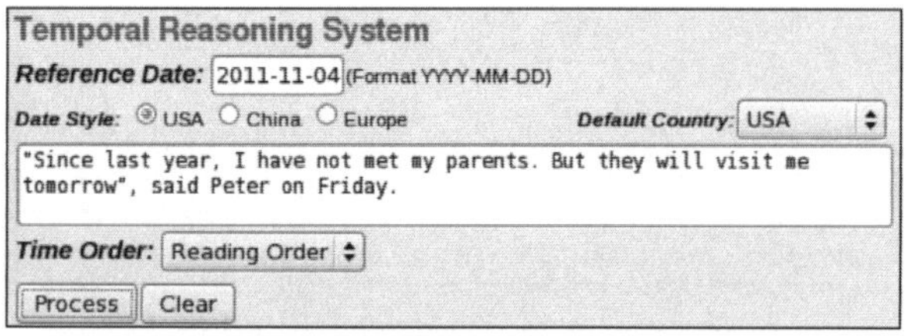

Figure 2: A screenshot of the input panel.

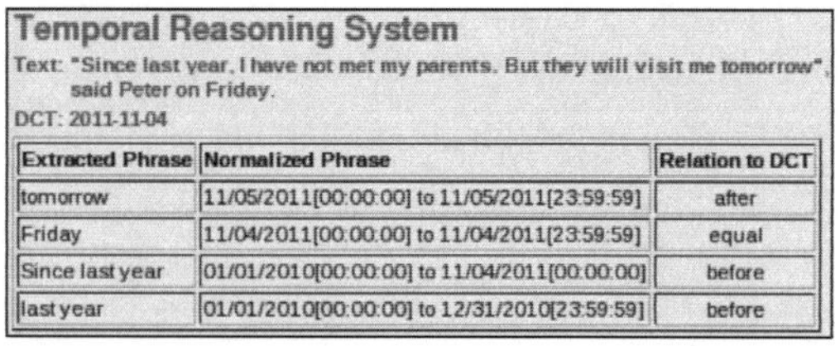

Extracted Phrase	Normalized Phrase	Relation to DCT
tomorrow	11/05/2011[00:00:00] to 11/05/2011[23:59:59]	after
Friday	11/04/2011[00:00:00] to 11/04/2011[23:59:59]	equal
Since last year	01/01/2010[00:00:00] to 11/04/2011[00:00:00]	before
last year	01/01/2010[00:00:00] to 12/31/2010[23:59:59]	before

Figure 3: A screenshot of the output panel.

4 The Demonstration

4.1 Visualization

We have implemented our system in a web-based demo[4]. Figure 2 shows a screenshot of the input panel of the system. The input panel includes a main text box that allows users to input the text, and some other input fields that allow users to customize the system's outputs. Among the fields, the reference date serves as the document creation time (DCT) of the input text. All temporal expressions captured from the text will be normalized based on the reference date and compared also to the reference date as illustrated in Figure 3.

4.2 Script Outline

First, we will give an overview of existing temporal reasoning systems. Then we will introduce the novel contributions of our system. After that, we will go over our web-based demonstration, including (i) the input panel: reference date and the text to be analyzed, and (ii) the output panel: the extracted basic and extended temporal expressions, the normalized intervals, and the comparison results.

5 Conclusions

In this demonstration paper, we introduced a temporal reasoning system that addresses three fundamental problems related to temporal expressions in text, including extraction, normalization and comparison. Our system consists of a temporal expression extractor capable of dealing with complex temporal phrases, a time interval normalizer and a time interval comparator. The experimental study shows that our system achieves a high level of performance, which will allow it to support other systems that require complicated temporal reasoning.

[4]http://cogcomp.cs.illinois.edu/page/demo_view/TempSys

Acknowledgement

This research is supported by the Army Research Laboratory (ARL) under agreement W911NF-09-2-0053 and the Defense Advanced Research Projects Agency (DARPA) Machine Reading Program under Air Force Research Laboratory (AFRL) prime contract no. FA8750-09-C-0181. The second author also thanks the Vietnam Education Foundation (VEF) for its sponsorship. Any opinions, findings, and conclusion or recommendations expressed in this material are those of the authors and do not necessarily reflect the view of the VEF, ARL, DARPA, AFRL, or the US government.

References

Omar Alonso, Jannik Strötgen, Ricardo Baeza-Yates, and Michael Gertz. 2011. Temporal information retrieval: Challenges and opportunities. In *TWAW*.

Eugene Charniak and Mark Johnson. 2005. Coarse-to-fine n-best parsing and maxent discriminative reranking. In *ACL*.

Heng Ji, Ralph Grishman, and Hoa Trang Dang. 2011. Overview of the tac2011 knowledge base population track. In *TAC*.

James Pustejovsky, Jose Castano, Robert Ingria, Roser Sauri, Robert Gaizauskas, Andrea Setzer, and Graham Katz. 2003. Timeml: Robust specification of event and temporal expressions in text. In *IWCS-5*.

D. Roth and D. Zelenko. 1998. Part of speech tagging using a network of linear separators. In *COLING-ACL, The 17th International Conference on Computational Linguistics*.

Jannik Strötgen and Michael Gertz. 2010. Heideltime: High quality rule-based extraction and normalization of temporal expressions. In *Proceedings of the 5th International Workshop on Semantic Evaluation*, SemEval '10.

Marc Verhagen, Roser Sauri, Tommaso Caselli, and James Pustejovsky. 2010. Semeval-2010 task 13: Tempeval-2. In *Proceedings of the 5th International Workshop on Semantic Evaluation*.

Yafang Wang, Mingjie Zhu, Lizhen Qu, Marc Spaniol, and Gerhard Weikum. 2010. Timely yago: harvesting, querying, and visualizing temporal knowledge from wikipedia. In *EDBT*.

AttitudeMiner: Mining Attitude from Online Discussions

Amjad Abu-Jbara
EECS Department
University of Michigan
Ann Arbor, MI, USA
amjbara@umich.edu

Ahmed Hassan
Microsoft Research
Redmond, WA, USA
hassanam@microsoft.com

Dragomir Radev
EECS Department
University of Michigan
Ann Arbor, MI, USA
radev@umich.edu

Abstract

This demonstration presents AttitudeMiner, a system for mining attitude from online discussions. AttitudeMiner uses linguistic techniques to analyze the text exchanged between participants of online discussion threads at different levels of granularity: the word level, the sentence level, the post level, and the thread level. The goal of this analysis is to identify the polarity of the attitude the discussants carry towards one another. Attitude predictions are used to construct a signed network representation of the discussion thread. In this network, each discussant is represented by a node. An edge connects two discussants if they exchanged posts. The sign (positive or negative) of the edge is set based on the polarity of the attitude identified in the text associated with the edge. The system can be used in different applications such as: word polarity identification, identifying attitudinal sentences and their signs, signed social network extraction from text, subgroup detect in discussion. The system is publicly available for download and has an online demonstration at http://clair.eecs.umich.edu/AttitudeMiner/.

1 Introduction

The rapid growth of social media has encouraged people to interact with each other and get involved in discussions more than anytime before. The most common form of interaction on the web uses text as the main communication medium. When people discuss a topic, especially when it is a controversial one, it is normal to see situations of both agreement and disagreement among the discussants. It is even not uncommon that the big group of discussants split into two or more smaller subgroups. The members of each subgroup mostly agree and show positive attitude toward each other, while they mostly disagree with the members of opposing subgroups and possibly show negative attitude toward them. These forms of sentiment are expressed in text by using certain language constructs (e.g. use insult or negative slang to express negative attitude).

In this demonstration, we present a system that applies linguistic analysis techniques to the text of online discussions to predict the polarity of relations that develop between discussants. This analysis is done on words to identify their polarities, then on sentences to identify attitudinal sentences and the sign of attitude, then on the post level to identify the sign of an interaction, and finally on the entire thread level to identify the overall polarity of the relation. Once the polarity of the pairwise relations that develop between interacting discussants is identified, this information is then used to construct a signed network representation of the discussion thread.

The system also implements two signed network partitioning techniques that can be used to detect how the discussants split into subgroups regarding the discussion topic.

The functionality of the system is based on our previous research on word polarity identification (Hassan and Radev, 2010) and attitude identification (Hassan et al., 2010). The system is publicly available for download and has a web interface to try online[1].

This work is related to previous work in the areas of sentiment analysis and online discussion mining. Many previous systems studied the problem of identifying the polarity of individual words (Hatzivassiloglou and McKeown, 1997; Turney and Littman, 2003). Opinionfinder (Wilson et al., 2005a) is a system for mining opinions from text. Another research line focused on analyzing online discussions. For example, Lin et al. (2009) proposed a sparse coding-based model that simultaneously models the semantics and the structure of threaded discussions and Shen et al. (2006) proposed a method for exploiting the temporal information in discussion streams to identify the reply structure of the dialog. Many systems addressed the problem of extracting social networks from data (Elson et al., 2010; McCallum et al., 2007), but none of them considered both positive and negative relations.

In the rest of the paper, we describe the system architecture, implementation, usage, and its perfor-

[1]http://clair.eecs.umich.edu/AttitudeMiner/

Proceedings of the NAACL-HLT 2012: Demonstration Session, pages 33–36,
Montréal, Canada, June 3-8, 2012.

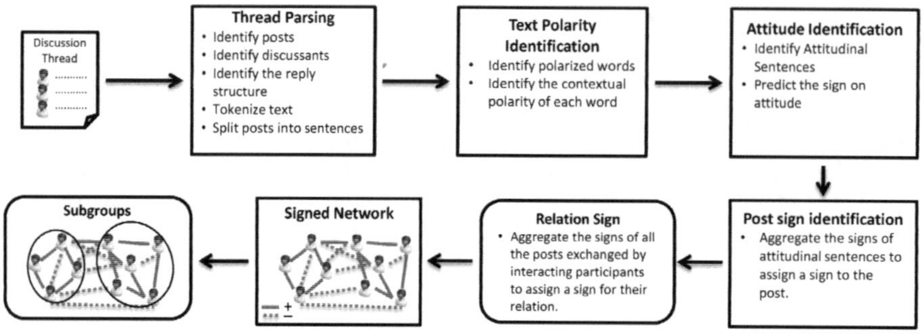

Figure 1: Overview of the system processing pipeline

mance evaluation.

2 System Overview

Figure 1 shows a block diagram of the system components and the processing pipeline. The first component in the system is the *thread parsing* component which takes as input a discussion thread and parses it to identify the posts, the participants, and the reply structure of the thread. This component uses a module from CLAIRLib (Abu-Jbara and Radev, 2011) to tokenize the posts and split them into sentences.

The second component in the pipeline processes the text of the posts to identify polarized words and tag them with their polarity. This component uses the publicly available tool, opinionfinder (Wilson et al., 2005a), as a framework for polarity identification. This component uses an extended polarity lexicon created by applying a random walk model to WordNet (Miller, 1995) and a set of seed polarized words. This approach is described in detail in our previous work (Hassan and Radev, 2010). The context of words is taken into consideration by running a contextual word classifier that determines whether the word is used in a polarized sense given the context (Wilson et al., 2005b). For example, a positive word appearing in a negated scope is used in a negative, rather than a positive sense.

The next component is the attitude identification component. Given a sentence, our model predicts whether it carries an attitude from the text writer toward the text recipient or not. As we are only interested in attitudes between participants, we limit our analysis to sentences that use mentions of a discussion participants (i.e. names or second person pronouns). We also discard all sentences that do not contain polarized expressions as detected by the previous component. We extract several patterns at different levels of generalization representing any given sentence. We use words, part-of-speech tags, and dependency relations. We use those patterns to build two Markov models for every kind of patterns. The first model characterizes the relation between different tokens for all patterns that correspond to sentences that have an attitude. The second model is similar to the first one, but it uses all patterns that correspond to sentences that do not have an attitude. Given a new sentence, we extract the corresponding patterns and estimate the likelihood of every pattern being generated from the two corresponding models. We then compute the likelihood ratio of the sentence under every pair of models. Notice that we have a pair of models corresponding to every type of patterns. The likelihood ratios are combined using a linear model, the parameters of which are estimated using a development dataset. Please refer to (Hassan et al., 2010) for more details about this component.

The next component works on the post level. It assigns a sign to each post based on the signs of the sentences it contains. A post is classified as negative if it has at least N_s negative sentences, otherwise it is classified as positive. The value of N_s can be chosen by the user or set to default which was estimated using a small labeled development set. The default value for N_s is 1 (i.e. if the post contains at least one negative sentence, the whole post is considered to be negative).

The next component in the pipeline uses the attitude predictions from posts to construct a signed network representation of the discussion thread. Each participant is represented by a node. An edge is created between two participants if they interacted with each other. A sign (positive or negative) is assigned to an edge based on the signs of the posts the two participants connected by the edge have exchanged. This is done by comparing the number of positive and negative posts. A negative sign is given if the two participants exchanged at least N_p negative posts. The value of N_p can be set using a development set. The default value is 1.

The last component is the subgroup identifica-

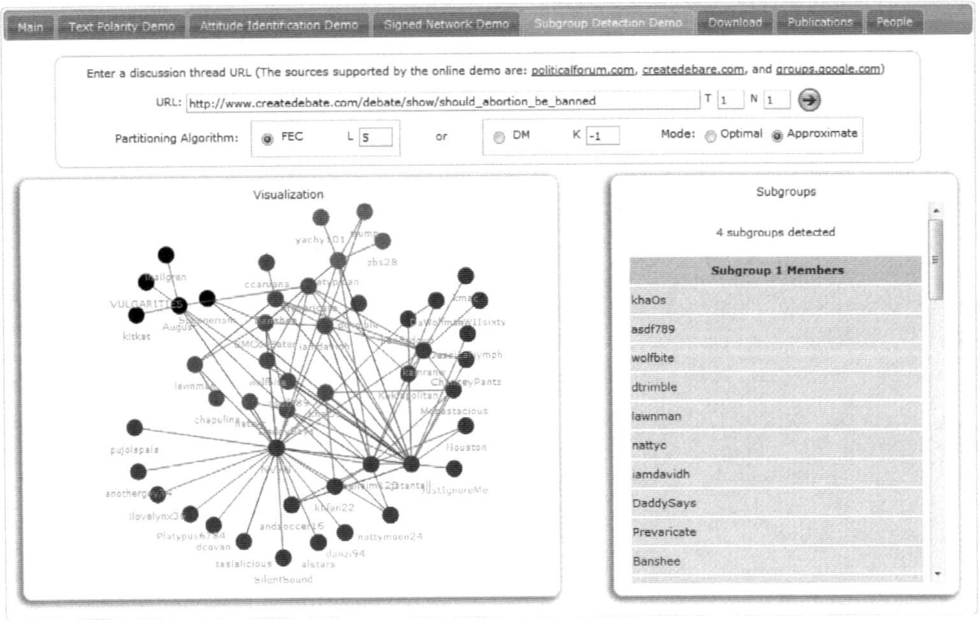

Figure 2: The web interface for detecting subgroups in discussions

tion component. This component provides implementations for two signed network partitioning algorithms. The first one is a greedy optimization algorithm that is based on the principals of the structural balance theory. The algorithm uses a criterion function for a local optimization partitioning such that positive links are dense within groups and negative links are dense between groups. The algorithm is described in detail in (Doreian and Mrvar, 1996). The second algorithm is FEC (Yang et al., 2007). FEC is based on an agent-based random walk model. It starts by finding a sink community, and then extracting it from the entire network based on a graph cut criteria that Yang et al. (2007) proposed. The same process is then applied recursively to the extracted community and the rest of the network.

3 Implementation Details

The system is implemented in Perl. Some of the components in the processing pipeline use external tools that are implemented in either Perl, Java, or Python. All the external tools come bundled with the system. The system is compatible with all the major platforms including windows, Mac OS, and all Linux distributions. The installation process is very straightforward. There is a single installation script that will install the system, install all the dependencies, and do all the required configurations. The installation requires that Java JRE, Perl, and Python be installed on the machine.

The system has a command-line interface that provides full access to the system functionality. The command-line interface can be used to run the whole pipeline or any portion of it. It can also be used to access any component directly. Each component has a corresponding script that can be run separately. The input and output specifications of each component are described in the accompanying documentation. All the parameters that control the performance of the system can also be passed through the command-line interface.

The system can process any discussion thread that is input to it in a specific XML format. The final output of the system is also in XML format. The XML schema of the input/output is described in the documentation. It is the user responsibility to write a parser that converts an online discussion thread to the expected XML format. The system package comes with three such parsers for three different discussion sites: www.politicalforum.com, groups.google.com, and www.createdebate.com.

The distribution also comes with three datasets (from three different sources) comprising a total of 300 discussion threads. The datasets are annotated with the subgroup labels of discussants. Included in the distribution as well, a script for generating a visualization of the extracted signed network and the identified subgroups.

AttitudeMiner also has a web interface that demonstrates most of its functionality. The web in-

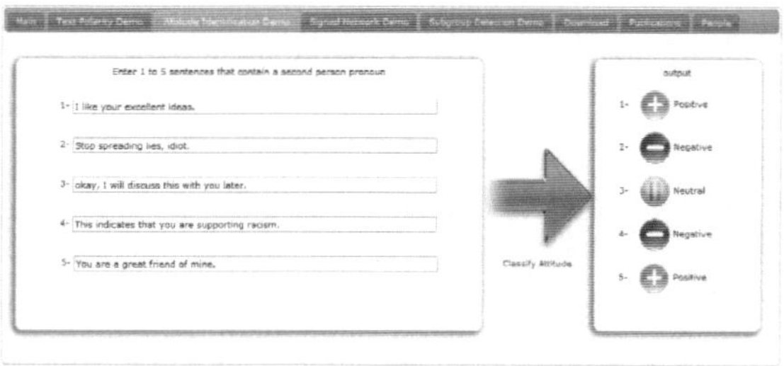

Figure 3: The web interface for identifying attitudinal sentences and their polarity

terface is intended for demonstration purposes only. No webservice is provided. Figure 2 and Figrue 3 show two screenshots for the web interface.

4 System Performance

In this section, we give a brief summary of the system performance. The method that generates the extended polarity lexicon that is used for word polarity identification achieves 88.8% accuracy as reported in (Hassan and Radev, 2010). The attitude identification component distinguishes between attitudinal and non-attitudinal sentences with 80.3% accuracy, and predicts the signs of attitudinal sentences with 97% accuracy as reported in (Hassan et al., 2010). Our evaluation for the signed network extraction component on a large annotated dataset showed that it achieves 83.5% accuracy. Finally, our experiments on an annotated discussion showed that the system can detect subgroups with 77.8% purity. The system was evaluated using a dataset with thousands of posts labeled by human annotators.

5 Conclusion

We presented of a demonstration of a social media mining system that used linguistic analysis techniques to understand the relations that develop between users in online communities. The system is capable of analyzing the text exchanged during discussions and identifying positive and negative attitudes. Positive attitude reflects a friendly relation while negative attitude is a sign of an antagonistic relation. The system can also use the attitude information to identify subgroups with a homogeneous and common focus among the discussants. The system predicts attitudes and identifies subgroups with high accuracy.

Acknowledgments

This research was funded by the Office of the Director of National Intelligence (ODNI), Intelligence Advanced Research Projects Activity (IARPA), through the U.S. Army Research Lab. All statements of fact, opinion or conclusions contained herein are those of the authors and should not be construed as representing the official views or policies of IARPA, the ODNI or the U.S. Government.

References

Amjad Abu-Jbara and Dragomir Radev. 2011. Clairlib: A toolkit for natural language processing, information retrieval, and network analysis. In *ACL-HLT 2011-Demo*, June.

Patrick Doreian and Andrej Mrvar. 1996. A partitioning approach to structural balance. *Social Networks*.

David Elson, Nicholas Dames, and Kathleen McKeown. 2010. Extracting social networks from literary fiction. In *ACL 2010*, pages 138–147, Uppsala, Sweden, July.

Ahmed Hassan and Dragomir R. Radev. 2010. Identifying text polarity using random walks. In *ACL 2010*.

Ahmed Hassan, Vahed Qazvinian, and Dragomir Radev. 2010. What's with the attitude? identifying sentences with attitude in online discussions.

Vasileios Hatzivassiloglou and Kathleen R. McKeown. 1997. Predicting the semantic orientation of adjectives. In *EACL'97*.

Chen Lin, Jiang-Ming Yang, Rui Cai, Xin-Jing Wang, and Wei Wang. 2009. Simultaneously modeling semantics and structure of threaded discussions: a sparse coding approach and its applications. In *SIGIR '09*.

Andrew McCallum, Xuerui Wang, and Andrés Corrada-Emmanuel. 2007. Topic and role discovery in social networks with experiments on enron and academic email. *J. Artif. Int. Res.*

George A. Miller. 1995. Wordnet: A lexical database for english. *Communications of the ACM*.

Dou Shen, Qiang Yang, Jian-Tao Sun, and Zheng Chen. 2006. Thread detection in dynamic text message streams. In *SIGIR '06*, pages 35–42.

Peter Turney and Michael Littman. 2003. Measuring praise and criticism: Inference of semantic orientation from association. *ACM Transactions on Information Systems*.

Theresa Wilson, Paul Hoffmann, Swapna Somasundaran, Jason Kessler, Janyce Wiebe, Yejin Choi, Claire Cardie, Ellen Riloff, and Siddharth Patwardhan. 2005a. Opinionfinder: a system for subjectivity analysis. In *HLT/EMNLP - Demo*.

Theresa Wilson, Janyce Wiebe, and Paul Hoffmann. 2005b. Recognizing contextual polarity in phrase-level sentiment analysis. In *HLT/EMNLP'05*.

Bo Yang, William Cheung, and Jiming Liu. 2007. Community mining from signed social networks. *IEEE Trans. on Knowl. and Data Eng.*

AUTHOR INDEX